Experiencing Music Composition in Middle School General Music

Experiencing Music Composition in Middle School General Music

Michele Kaschub and Janice P. Smith

Published in partnership with
National Association for Music Education

ROWMAN & LITTLEFIELD
Lanham • Boulder • New York • London

Published in partnership with National Association for Music Education

Published by Rowman & Littlefield
An imprint of The Rowman & Littlefield Publishing Group, Inc.
4501 Forbes Boulevard, Suite 200, Lanham, Maryland 20706
www.rowman.com

86-90 Paul Street, London EC2A 4NE

Copyright © 2022 by Michele Kaschub and Janice P. Smith

All rights reserved. No part of this book may be reproduced in any form or by any electronic or mechanical means, including information storage and retrieval systems, without written permission from the publisher, except by a reviewer who may quote passages in a review.

British Library Cataloguing in Publication Information Available

Library of Congress Cataloging-in-Publication Data

Names: Kaschub, Michele, 1967- author. | Smith, Janice P., author.
Title: Experiencing music composition in middle school general music / Michele Kaschub and Janice P. Smith.
Description: Lanham : Rowman & Littlefield, 2022. | Includes index. | Summary: "Experiencing Music Composition in Middle School General Music features pedagogical strategies and practical advice for teachers coupled with 15 engaging lessons tailored to meet the needs and interests of middle school musicians"—Provided by publisher.
Identifiers: LCCN 2022015230 (print) | LCCN 2022015231 (ebook) | ISBN 9781475864618 (cloth) | ISBN 9781475864625 (paperback) | ISBN 9781475864632 (epub)
Subjects: LCSH: Composition (Music)—Instruction and study | Music—Instruction and study—Outlines, syllabi, etc. | Middle school education.
Classification: LCC MT40 .K278 2022 (print) | LCC MT40 (ebook) | DDC 372.87/4—dc23/eng/20220405
LC record available at https://lccn.loc.gov/2022015230
LC ebook record available at https://lccn.loc.gov/2022015231

Contents

About the Companion Website ... vii

Introduction ... ix

SECTION 1: TEACHING AND LEARNING WITH *EXPERIENCING MUSIC COMPOSITION* ... 1

1. The *Experiencing Music Composition* Program ... 3
   Experiencing Music Composition and the National Arts Standards for Music ... 3
   Teaching Music Composition with the National Arts Standards for Music ... 4

2. What to Expect from Middle School Composers ... 9
   Typical Characteristics of Middle School Composers ... 9
   Typical Qualities of Compositions Created by Middle School Composers ... 10

3. How to Use This Book ... 11

SECTION 2: FACILITATING THE WORK OF MIDDLE SCHOOL COMPOSERS ... 13

4. Compositional Capacities ... 15
   On Composing ... 15
   Compositional Capacities ... 15
   Feelingful Intention ... 15
      Developing the Capacity of Feelingful Intention ... 16
   Musical Expressivity ... 16
      More about the MUSTS ... 18
      Developing the Capacity of Musical Expressivity ... 19
   Artistic Craftsmanship ... 20
      Techniques and Études for Grades 6–8 ... 21
      Developing the Capacity of Artistic Craftsmanship ... 26
   Final Thoughts ... 26

5. Using *Sketchpages* ... 27
   Guiding the Journey ... 27
   Introducing *Sketchpages* to Middle School Composers ... 28
   Sketchpages as Multitaskers ... 31

SECTION 3: CREATIVE POSITIVE COMPOSITIONAL EXPERIENCES ... 33

6. Composition Requires a Different Kind of Teaching ... 35
   Working with "In-process" Composers ... 37
   Anchoring Knowledge, Inviting Inspiration ... 38

	Guidelines for Sharing Compositions—Giving and Receiving Feedback	39
	Making the Most of Limited Timeframes	44

SECTION 4: TEACHER GUIDES AND STUDENT *SKETCHPAGES* — 45

7	Teacher Guides	47
	Curricular Organization	47

Projects for Beginning Composers — 49

8	*Songwriting*—A Songwriter's Workshop	51
9	*Film Scoring*—And Now, A Public Service Announcement	59
10	*Instrumental Music*—Percussing Art	65
11	*Electronic Music & Digital Media*—Light Up Your Phone with a Bespoke Ringtone	69
12	*Music Theater*—Color Me Moody!	73

Projects for Intermediate Composers — 77

13	*Songwriting*—Haiku Opera	79
14	*Film Scoring*—One Scene, Many Interpretations	91
15	*Instrumental Music*—Upcycled Music	97
16	*Electronic Music & Digital Media*—Song Production	105
17	*Music Theater*—Spoken Word & Music	113

Projects for Advanced Composers — 119

18	*Songwriting*—Creating a Jazz Vocal	121
19	*Film Scoring*—Scoring Dynamic Documentaries	129
20	*Instrumental Music*—Composing Idiomatic Solos	141
21	*Electronic Music & Digital Media*—Environmental Musics	149
22	*Music Theater*—Reimagining Great Literature	159

Appendix A: Notation Templates	165
Appendix B: Critical Reflection and Composer Feedback Guides	169
Index	171
About the Authors	173

About the Companion Website

https://rowman.com/ISBN/9781475864618/Experiencing-Music-Composition-in-Middle-School-General-Music

Rowman & Littlefield has created a website to accompany *Experiencing Music Composition in Middle School General Music*. Full-color versions of each *Sketchpage* are provided so that teachers may project these images when facilitating classroom instruction or guiding whole-class composition activities. Black and white versions for printing and distribution to students are also provided.

Introduction

Welcome to *Experiencing Music Composition*

Composing music can be a wonderful experience for adolescents. It allows them to discover their musical imaginations as they create songs and other musical works to suit their needs and interests and which they can share with others. Often people think that young musicians need extensive formal training in music theory or considerable skill as performers to compose, but we have found that just about everyone can create music with a little help and some useful strategies. This book offers exactly that. It provides guidance for teachers who are ready to nurture creative spirits and suggests tools young composers can use both in school and at home to capture and manage their many musical ideas.

You do not have to be a professional composer to guide students as they create their own music, but some formal music training can be helpful. Active listening skills, a willingness to explore and consider a broad range of musical possibilities, some practice at asking critical questions of young composers about their work, and a strong belief that music will emerge from what may appear to be a busy, messy, and sometimes rather loud sound environment are all you need. These skills and dispositions, combined with a focused approach, will allow you and your students to find musical satisfaction and ongoing success.

In the following sections, we will introduce the *Experiencing Music Composition* approach and present a snapshot of middle school composers and their work across Grades 6–8. The teaching and learning tools of *Experiencing Music Composition* can be used by composers of all ages to develop capacities critical to creating original music. Three capacities—*feelingful intention*, *musical expressivity*, and *artistic craftsmanship*—provide the springboard that advances children's work from collections of random sounds and brief musical gestures to thoughtfully created, expressive pieces. *Sketchpages* are graphic organizers that guide students in thinking through their compositional ideas. They are included with every lesson to support the development of musical artistry. Each lesson also includes suggestions for productive sharing and feedback in a variety of formats to help composers assess their progress and evaluate the quality of their work.

We are delighted that you and your middle school students are embarking on an exciting journey in creating original music, and we hope that you will love *Experiencing Music Composition*.

Michele Kaschub

Janice P. Smith

Section 1

TEACHING AND LEARNING WITH
EXPERIENCING MUSIC COMPOSITION

Chapter 1

The *Experiencing Music Composition* Program

Experiencing Music Composition is focused on providing opportunities for K–12 students to create original music through composition. The approach progresses from teacher-facilitated collaborative work, through partnered and small group activities, toward projects where the students assume complete artistic autonomy. The lessons and activities of the program are designed to challenge students' skills and understandings as they explore the expressive potentials of sound across different genres, settings, and media.

The *Experiencing Music Composition* program is suitable for use in private teaching studios, school music programs, and any other place where young people make music. The compositional tasks of the program parallel those undertaken by singer-songwriters, movie score composers, video game score composers, commercial jingles creators, and everything in between. Students create songs, works for chorus and instrumental ensembles, pieces partnered with electronic media, music to accompany art installations, film, music theater, and much, much more.

Graphic organizers, called *Sketchpages*, guide and enhance this work. Designed specifically to promote student creativity and develop key compositional skills, *Sketchpages* are a mix of doodle space and a composer's sketchbook. As students work with these pages, they are invited to imagine how their music might sound and how others may experience those sounds as performers and listeners. Students quickly learn to identify and develop the feelings, thoughts, and ideas they wish to explore and share through their work. Furthermore, they learn to use the tools and techniques of composition expressively to achieve artistic ends.

Experiencing Music Composition promotes individuality. Students are encouraged to create music in a manner that reveals their unique musical ideas. This signature sound is often referred to as the composer's "voice." Just as many musical listeners easily recognize works of Aaron Copland, Louis Armstrong, the Jonas Brothers, or Beyoncé, so will members of your musical community be able to identify pieces that "belong" to a specific composer or group of collaborative composers. The emergence of "voice" is important because it reveals a clarity of music thought and the capacity to engage meaningfully with music over time.

While individual voice is an important development for any artist, isolation rarely leads to meaningful growth. The *Experiencing Music Composition* program emphasizes collaborative learning, facilitated sharing, and productive feedback through Composer's Circles—a forum in which composers may share their work and ask other members of the community for reactions, advice, and suggestions. As composers interact with peers, teachers, performers, and others from the musical community-at-large, they are exposed to a broad palette of compositional tools, techniques and ideas that may shape or influence not only their current project, but future projects as well. This social format provides an important counterpart to work that may be isolating and helps composers balance subjective and objective evaluations of their own work.

EXPERIENCING MUSIC COMPOSITION AND THE NATIONAL ARTS STANDARDS FOR MUSIC

The lessons and activities of the *Experiencing Music Composition* program can work seamlessly with the *National Core Arts Standards*.[1] Each lesson touches upon the Enduring Understandings and Essential Questions outlined within the standards while leaving the specific path to learning open. This kind of music learning is personally relevant and driven by each student's curiosities and passions within music. The compositional challenges that students face are authentic and true to the experience of composition in the world at large.

More specifically, composition allows students to explore their creative ideas, concepts, and feeling through the creation of music that represents their unique artistic perspectives. Drawing on a variety of sources and influences, composers engage with perceptual and conceptual knowledge to imagine music for a variety of purposes. Composers use their previous experiences and emerging expertise to develop expressive intent. As they set feelingful intentions and engage in artistic craftsmanship, they enter an exciting process of testing, evaluating, selecting, and refining their musical ideas. When the work is finished, composers may decide to present it to others.

However, not all compositions will be shared with an audience. For some composers and some composition activities, performance is not the goal. Some composers write only for themselves. Even with encouragement from others to share what they have composed, they may choose not to do so. This choice represents a process of selection, analysis, and evaluation in which the student has decided not to make a particular work public. If and when composers choose to share their music, either by performing it themselves or through the performance of others, they will need to select, analyze, interpret, rehearse, evaluate, refine, and present their creations in the role of performer or as the advisor to the performers.

Composers are often influenced by what they hear in the music of other composers. Moreover, as they listen to the work of others, composers select, analyze, interpret, and evaluate what they hear. They respond to selected influences by analyzing them and by using those influences in their own works. This is especially true of young composers who are learning to craft feelingful sounds. "I want to compose something like that" is a common reaction to music that has made a feelingful impact on them.

Finally, composition provides a way for students to connect their personal interests, experiences, and ideas to musical sounds. In doing so, they deepen their understanding of all aspects of creating, performing, and responding because all three actions must be considered by the composer. The ability to synthesize and relate experience and sound can be developed in students. The *National Arts Standards* provide curricular guidelines for this work. The *Experiencing Music Composition* approach, with its emphasis on the development of feelingful intention, musical expressivity, and artistic craftsmanship, offers teachers strategies for welcoming composition into their classrooms.

TEACHING MUSIC COMPOSITION WITH THE NATIONAL ARTS STANDARDS FOR MUSIC

In compositional work, the artistic process and learning must belong to the student. If teachers can predict that everyone will learn the same technique or have the same experience, then they are engaging students with études. Études are a particular type of compositional activity in which the teacher controls the artistic process for the express purpose of introducing students to a new technique or musical practice (For étude examples, see pages 21–26). These activities are of value because they present specific aspects of artistic craftsmanship and music theory. However, they should not be confused with composing music.

Composition is an emergent process where students' artistic autonomy is critical. As students compose, they must be able to make musical and artistic choices that are meaningful within their understanding of music. The composition activities outlined in this book provide teachers with an opportunity to gently guide—rather than predict—product outcomes. The process and the resulting products must be student-centered and student-driven. Consequently, students may meet different standards at different times.

While the standards provide guidelines, individual expressivity and voice are the goals of composing. The *Experiencing Music Composition* approach provides teachers with the opportunity to truly tailor instruction to the needs of individual students. However, emergent learning can be a challenge to document. To help teachers manage this process, we suggest creating a standards checklist for each student. One possible example of this is shown in figures 1.1–1.3. This type of formative assessment can be used to inform future instruction.

Student Name_____

In the boxes, note the date and in which project or lesson you notice the student exhibiting these behaviors.

Standards 6	Emerging	Approaches	Meets	Exceeds
Generate simple rhythmic, melodic, and harmonic phrases within AB and ABA forms that convey expressive intent.				
MU:Cr2.1.6a Select, organize, construct, and document personal musical ideas for arrangements and compositions within AB or ABA form that demonstrate an effective beginning, middle, and ending, and convey expressive intent.				
MU:Cr2.1.6b Use standard and/or iconic notation and/or audio/ video recording to document personal simple rhythmic phrases, melodic phrases, and two-chord harmonic musical ideas.				
MU:Cr3.1.6a Evaluate their own work, applying teacher-provided criteria such as application of selected elements of music, and use of sound sources.				
MU:Cr3.1.6b Describe the rationale for making revisions to the music based on evaluation criteria and feedback from their teacher.				
MU:Cr3.2.6a Present the final version of their documented personal composition or arrangement, using craftsmanship and originality to demonstrate an effective beginning, middle, and ending, and convey expressive intent.				

Figure 1.1 National Arts Standards for Music, Creating, Grade 6. *Source*: Adapted by Michele Kaschub and Janice P. Smith from the 2014 National Core Arts Standards, State Education Agency Directors of Arts Education.

Student Name _____

In the boxes, note the date and in which project or lesson you notice the student exhibiting these behaviors.

Standards 7	Emerging	Approaches	Meets	Exceeds
MU:Cr1.1.7a Generate rhythmic, melodic, and harmonic phrases and variations over harmonic accompaniments within AB, ABA, or theme and variation forms that convey expressive intent.				
MU:Cr2.1.7a Select, organize, develop and document personal musical ideas for arrangements, songs, and compositions within AB, ABA, or theme and variation forms that demonstrate unity and variety and convey expressive intent.				
MU:Cr2.1.7b Use standard and/or iconic notation and/or audio/ video recording to document personal simple rhythmic phrases, melodic phrases, and harmonic sequences.				
MU:Cr3.1.7a Evaluate their own work, applying selected criteria such as appropriate application of elements of music including style, form, and use of sound sources.				
MU:Cr3.1.7b Describe the rationale for making revisions to the music based on evaluation criteria and feedback from others (teacher and peers).				
MU:Cr3.2.7a Present the final version of their documented personal composition, song, or arrangement, using craftsmanship and originality to demonstrate unity and variety, and convey expressive intent.				

Figure 1.2 National Arts Standards for Music, Creating, Grade 7. *Source*: Adapted by Michele Kaschub and Janice P. Smith from the 2014 National Core Arts Standards, State Education Agency Directors of Arts Education.

Student Name_____

In the boxes, note the date and in which project or lesson you notice the student exhibiting these behaviors.

Standards 8	Emerging	Approaches	Meets	Exceeds
MU:Cr1.1.8a Generate rhythmic, melodic and harmonic phrases and harmonic accompaniments within expanded forms (including introductions, transitions, and codas) that convey expressive intent.				
MU:Cr2.1.8a Select, organize, and document personal musical ideas for arrangements, songs, and compositions within expanded forms that demonstrate tension and release, unity and variety, balance, and convey expressive intent.				
MU:Cr2.1.8b Use standard and/or iconic notation and/or audio/ video recording to document personal rhythmic phrases, melodic phrases, and harmonic sequences.				
MU:Cr3.1.8a Evaluate their own work by selecting and applying criteria including appropriate application of compositional techniques, style, form, and use of sound sources.				
MU:Cr3.1.8b Describe the rationale for refining works by explaining the choices, based on evaluation criteria.				
MU:Cr3.2.8a Present the final version of their documented personal composition, song, or arrangement, using craftsmanship and originality to demonstrate the application of compositional techniques for creating unity and variety, tension and release, and balance to convey expressive intent.				

Figure 1.3 National Arts Standards for Music, Creating, Grade 8. *Source*: Adapted by Michele Kaschub and Janice P. Smith from the 2014 National Core Arts Standards, State Education Agency Directors of Arts Education.

NOTE

1. The 2014 *National Core Arts Standards* are available from State Education Agency Directors of Arts Education (SEADAE) at https://www.nationalartsstandards.org.

Chapter 2

What to Expect from Middle School Composers

Middle school composers often feel a deep sense of ownership and pride in their work. Their musical creations are uniquely personal and important to them as they reflect their lived experiences and beliefs. The weight of this meaning-laden work, coupled with the dynamic landscape of physical, emotional, and social changes that are the hallmark of adolescence, requires the creation of welcoming, safe spaces for artistic work. The composing classroom or workspace must be one where all ideas are accepted and where trying new things and sharing music is expected. This is the type of open environment where meaningful learning can take place.

Composers throughout history share many characteristics, but there are also attributes that are specific to different stages of human and musical development. The following descriptions of middle school composers—their working styles and their music—may be helpful in determining what is appropriate and useful in guiding their work.

TYPICAL CHARACTERISTICS OF MIDDLE SCHOOL COMPOSERS

- Middle school composers are guardedly curious about how music works and what they might create.
- Middle school composers may see themselves as able to develop skills to accomplish their musical intentions or as limited to what they can currently do.[1]
- Middle school composers are musically intuitive and draw on a broad range of previous formal and informal musical experiences as they work.
- Middle school composers are eager to manipulate sounds that intrigue them and often prefer to work with guitars, keyboards, drums, computers or smart devices, or other instruments that they are currently studying.
- Middle school composers benefit from exposure to compositional models.
- Middle school composers need experiences as listeners, performers, and composers to fully grasp how these three roles impact the creation of music.
- Middle school composers desire a balance between rules (guidelines that provide a conceptual framework and sense of safety) and freedoms (musical and artistic autonomy).
- Middle school composers benefit from peer interaction.
- Middle school composers learn from explaining and defending their musical ideas when respectfully challenged by their peers.
- Middle school composers are able to imagine what feelings different people might experience in a variety of situations and how those feelings might sound as music.
- Middle school composers are able to match sound ideas with feelingful impressions.
- Middle school composers best acquire and retain the tools and techniques of composition on a "need to know" basis.
- Middle school composers may be either eager or hesitant to share their work, as sharing music exposes the composer's thinking and feeling to others.

- Middle school composers seek peer approval and may be very disappointed or even hurt if they do not receive it.
- Middle school composers may not share their true impressions, opinions, or feelings about their work or the work of others until a truly open and safe learning environment has been established.
- Middle school composers desire success, but often prefer not to "shine" too brightly.

TYPICAL QUALITIES OF COMPOSITIONS CREATED BY MIDDLE SCHOOL COMPOSERS

- Compositions tend to be rather conventional and typically fit into genres preferred by peers.
- Compositions created by students in the dual role of composer-performer will be limited by the technical proficiency of the "performer" and may not truly reflect the intentions of the "composer."
- Early compositions are often reflective of the composer's present emotional state; therefore, projects that span several class periods or working sessions may reveal several emotional states. Compositions created by more advanced composers will exhibit more consistency in feelingful intention.
- Compositions are often busy and crafted with lots of sound and movement. Silence and slow, sustained sounds can feel uncertain or be overly exposing for less experienced composers.
- Clear formal structures will be apparent in most works. Unless challenged to pursue different forms, vocal compositions will follow popular song forms, and instrumental music will tend toward through-composed or ABA organizations.

NOTE

1. This statement relates to psychological theories of "possible selves." Please see Oyserman, D. (2015). Identity-Based Motivation. *Emerging Trends in the Social and Behavioral Sciences: An Interdisciplinary, Searchable, and Linkable Resource*, Edited by Robert Scott and Stephen Kosslyn. John Wiley & Sons; Brinthaupt, T. M., & Lipka, R. P. (Eds.). (2012). *Understanding Early Adolescent Self and Identity: Applications and Interventions*. Suny Press; and Varvarigou, M., Creech, A., & Hallam, S. (2014). Partnership working and possible selves in music education. *International Journal of Music Education*, 32(1), 84–97.

Chapter 3

How to Use This Book

Table 3.1 Structural Organization of This Book

Section 1 *Experiencing Music Composition* and Middle School Composers	Section 2 Facilitating Composition and Using Sketchpages
Section 3 Creating Positive Compositional Experiences	Section 4 Teacher Guides and Student *Sketchpages*

Source: Created by Michele Kaschub and Janice P. Smith.

This book is divided into four sections. Each section offers insights and tools for working with young composers. Sections 1–3 are designed to prepare educators to teach composition. Section 4 provides suggestions for implementing specific lessons.

Section 1 introduces the key focus on the *Experiencing Music Composition* approach—the three compositional capacities that are the foundation of the composer's work. Numerous examples and resources are provided to prepare teachers to guide students as they develop specific skills and abilities related to each compositional capacity.

Section 2 focuses on facilitating the work of middle school composers and the use of *Sketchpages*. These graphic organizers serve as creative spaces and written guides for students to use when planning compositions, actively composing, or reflecting on their work. *Sketchpages* can be used to organize group work or to help individual composers as they consider the music they wish to create. *Sketchpages* can also be useful data-collection tools as they reveal the connections that students make between the three compositional capacities.

Creating music requires a deeply personal investment of self. Sharing music with others places young composers in a vulnerable position. Section 3 offers guidance and strategies for sharing work, providing feedback, and encouraging future growth in a manner that fosters a positive learning environment and honors each composer's musical autonomy.

Ready to compose some music? Section 4 contains teacher guides with ready-to-use *Sketchpages* to get you and your middle school composers creating original music in five different compositional genres. Each guide outlines one or more possible approaches to the lesson. They are intended to help you get started and to serve as models as you develop your own composition projects suitable for any learning environment.

Section 2

FACILITATING THE WORK OF MIDDLE SCHOOL COMPOSERS

Chapter 4

Compositional Capacities

ON COMPOSING

All students have the ability to create music that is uniquely their own. The act of composing transcends the limits of verbal and mathematical representations and allows young people to explore sound as a means of sharing who they are, what they think, and what they feel about their experiences in the world. It invites them to draw on the full breadth of their musical skills and understanding to create music that represents their unique insights. As such, composition is more than just an activity of music education; it is a process that draws together intellect and intuition, thinking and feeling, and the practical and the inspired. It brings into reality thoughts and feelings that have only existed in the imagination and contributes to the creation of our individual and collective human spirit.

COMPOSITIONAL CAPACITIES

Just as some students find spelling easier than others—or read with greater comprehension or solve math problems more quickly—some young people will have a more developed sense of music composition than others. Students' abilities depend on their natural aptitude as well as the opportunities and the instruction they have had. Throughout *Experiencing Music Composition* activities will focus on the development of three compositional capacities: feelingful intention, musical expressivity, and artistic craftsmanship. Each plays an integral role in the way music is experienced and understood.

FEELINGFUL INTENTION

Middle school students often create musical motifs or short, repetitive pieces as they interact with their friends and classmates. Teachers who recognize and welcome these fledgling compositions can encourage composers to create more of them. As students develop music beyond these initial ideas, they can be guided to think about how their music makes them feel and how it might make others feel. To imagine the potential emotional impact of musical sounds is the capacity of *feelingful intention*.

Adolescents know that music has the ability to communicate because they have encountered music that has aroused their feelings. Simply suggesting to a composer that they create some music that conveys the impression of a familiar feeling can lead to compositions that are more expressive. For example, a group of seventh graders enters the music classroom huddled together in a conspiratorial laughter. The teacher listens to their emerging social plans and recognizes their excitement as a starting point for composing. The teacher suggests that the students create music about the theme park that they have just been talking about. Some of the students immediately engage in idea generation by listing the activities they have planned for the coming weekend. Phones and tablets appear and instruments are gathered as small groups begin exploring musical ideas. The teacher hears bass lines, rising and falling melodies with emerging lyrics, some simple harmonies, and the occasional digitized vocal. When the students share their pieces, each of these techniques will be identified and added to an ongoing list of compositional tools that can be used by composers to invite particular feelingful responses.

Developing the Capacity of Feelingful Intention

The intention to create music that sounds like feelings feel is implicit in all music. It is the *why* of music composition and the gateway to using compositional tools and techniques with artistic purpose. Young musicians are aware of the feelingful impact of the music that they encounter, but their awareness can be more tacit than explicit. Below are some activities that may be used to help students develop the capacity of feelingful intention.

1. Ask students to describe the feeling they get when they listen to a particular piece of music. Follow up with "What about the music makes you feel that way?" Remind the students that well-crafted music can invite different responses, so there may be many different answers and explanations.
2. Build a chart of words that can be used to describe moods, feelings, and impressions. A sample is shown in table 4.1, but students will have a greater ownership in a resource that they create and will reference it more frequently than they will do with a teacher handout or pre-made poster.
3. Encourage students to experiment with different intentions when they perform. If a single phrase is played with opposite intentions, does the nature of the music and/or their feelings about it change? In what way(s)?
4. Invite students to spend 10–15 minutes listening to and analyzing one of their own playlists. Do they notice a common feelingful intention? A string of related intentions? A highly varied set of feelingful intentions? What do they think about what they have observed? Does a similar list of feelingful intention descriptors fit the music they have composed? Why or why not?
5. Play "feelingful intention grab bag." Write feelingful intention descriptors on small pieces of paper and have students draw them out of a paper bag. Have students spend 2–5 minutes composing a short melodic idea that they believe captures the feeling of the descriptive word. Have the students perform their mini-composition for the whole group or for a partner and explain what they did in trying to invite a particular feelingful response.
6. Composers often write verbal introductions to pieces or may have left letters or other written documents describing their work. Share some of these with students after listening to the referenced piece. In what ways did the students' experiences of the piece match or differ from what the composer had intended?
7. Encourage students to identify the feelingful intention or intentions in their own work as well as in the work of their peers during sharing and reflection sessions.

Feelingful intentions may be outlined in planning stages of the compositional process or may also emerge organically as students explore and test many musical ideas as a piece unfolds. Regardless of the timing of its appearance, building an awareness of feelingful intention and its role in shaping musical decision-making is a key component in the artistic development of young composers.

MUSICAL EXPRESSIVITY

Music's expressive power relies on our ability to perceive the continually shifting balances within and between motion and stasis, unity and variety, sound and silence, tension and release, and stability and instability. These five musical principles, which we term "MUSTS," correspond directly to the way we perceive changes in our condition and environment through the complex array of our internal and external senses. When students understand this connection, they learn to reference their own intuitive understandings. They can draw on a personal bank of feelings that have arisen in their own experiences to consider how sound might be shaped to invite similar feelings in others. This skill allows composers to strategically select and shape how feelings are *sonified*—expressed in sound.

Continuing with the theme park example, some students might recall the excitement of the first time they were dropped off at a theme park and got to meet up with a group of friends without direct parental supervision (a mixture of excitement and nervous tension). Students may recall the relief they felt once they entered the park and connected with their friends (release).

Table 4.1 Words for Describing Feelingful Intentions

adorable	dramatic	hot	nasty	scary	tough
adventurous	dreary	huge	naughty	scratchy	tragic
afraid	dull	humble	needy	serene	tricky
amazing	eager	hungry	negative	serious	trusting
amused	electric	icky	nervous	sharp	ugly
angry	elegant	imaginative	nice	shimmering	understated
anxious	embarrassed	impish	numb	shiny	unique
awesome	enchanted	important	nutty	shrill	united
awful	energetic	impossible	odd	shy	unlucky
awkward	envious	innocent	orderly	sick	unpleasant
beautiful	evil	intelligent	ornate	silent	unruly
bold	exciting	irritating	outlandish	silly	unsteady
boring	exotic	jagged	overjoyed	simple	upset
bossy	fabulous	jazzy	overlooked	sizzling	useful
bouncy	fancy	jealous	pale	sleepy	vast
brave	fantastic	jittery	passionate	slow	velvety
bright	fast	jolly	peaceful	small	vibrant
broken	fat	joyous	perky	smooth	vicious
bubbly	feisty	jumpy	pesky	sneaky	victorious
bumpy	flowery	kind	plain	soft	villainous
busy	fluffy	klutzy	playful	somber	violent
calm	fluid	kooky	pompous	soulful	vivacious
careful	forceful	lazy	posh	stiff	vivid
charming	formal	light	powerful	stormy	warlike
cheerful	fresh	little	precious	strange	warm
clever	friendly	lively	pretty	strident	wary
clumsy	frightened	lonely	prickly	strong	watery
cold	funny	lopsided	proud	sturdy	wavy
confident	fussy	loud	pushy	stylish	weak
comfortable	fuzzy	loving	puzzled	surprised	weary
confused	gentle	low	quaint	sweet	weepy
courageous	giant	loyal	quarrelsome	sympathetic	weighty
creepy	glamorous	lucky	quick	tame	weird
crisp	glittering	lumpy	quiet	tedious	wet
crowded	gloomy	mad	quirky	tempting	whimsical
cruel	gorgeous	magnificent	radiant	tender	wicked
cuddly	graceful	majestic	ragged	tense	wide
curly	grateful	marvelous	rapid	terrible	wiggly
curvy	gross	massive	reckless	terrific	wild
cute	gruesome	mean	regal	thankful	wise
dangerous	grumpy	meek	reliable	thick	witty
daring	happy	mellow	rich	thin	wobbly
dark	harsh	memorable	rigid	thorny	woeful
deep	haunting	menacing	robust	thoughtful	wonderful
defiant	heavy	merry	rough	thunderous	young
delicate	high	messy	rowdy	tidy	youthful
delightful	hollow	misty	royal	tight	yummy
dizzy	hopeful	murky	sad	tiny	zany
dope	horrible	mysterious	safe	tired	zesty

Source: Created by Michele Kaschub and Janice P. Smith.

More about the MUSTS

The five principle pairs that comprise the MUSTS can be found in a wide variety of musics. While one or more of the principle pairs may be more prominent than others in a given work or section of a piece, all five are usually present in varying degree. Beyond presence or absence, it is the perception of the change in relational balance within each pair that gives rise to music's expressive potential. It is helpful to imagine each pair as situated on opposite ends of a continuum.

Motion and Stasis

People move in lots of different ways. They can climb, walk quickly, jump, run, amble or meander. Eventually, they will pause or even completely stop. Music, too, may contain moments of great motion, moments of stasis, and moments that are the degrees in between. If we were to use a slider to represent the relational balance for a piece with an A section of running sixteenth notes, it might look like figure 4.1.

Figure 4.1 Relational Balance Favoring Rhythmic Motion. *Source*: Created by Michele Kaschub and Janice P. Smith.

A slower moving B section, might be better represented as shown in figure 4.2.

Figure 4.2 Relational Balance Favoring Rhythmic Stasis. *Source*: Created by Michele Kaschub and Janice P. Smith.

Most important, the A and B sections are perceived to have more rhythmic motion or stasis through comparison to each other. These comparisons are not limited to those made within a single piece, but extend to all of the other musical pieces that a listener knows and can reference. It is also important to remember that rhythm constitutes just one type of motion-stasis pairing. Any of the musical elements can be crafted to influence how motion and stasis are experienced.

Unity and Variety

People look for patterns in nearly everything. The brain not only finds repetition to be highly satisfying but also seeks novelty to hold its attention in a different way. Most music uses a balance of unity and variety to create comfort as well as pique and hold our interest. While unity and variety can be achieved through any of music's components, striking just the right balance can be tricky. Too much of the same thing may cause a listener to lose interest, just as too many novel ideas may be overwhelming.

Sound and Silence

Sound is ubiquitous in daily life, yet the presence or absence of a particular sound can define the focus of our attention. In some cases, a single type of sound can become so familiar that it begins to function as an "attentional constant." Air-circulation devices, humming lights, passing traffic, and other environmental sounds are examples of sounds we often ignore until we notice their absence. In this way, silence plays an important role, as it can provide an opportunity to reframe and prioritize what is being heard.

Consider these two graphic representations of sound (gray) and silence (white). In the upper half of figure 4.3, a brass quintet delivers sound and silence in opposition so that the actions of the group are perceived as a whole. In the lower half of the figure, a shifting balance between sound and silence appears in the Trumpet 2 line against constant sound from the other members of the quintet. This structure may draw the listener to pay closer attention to the ideas delivered by the second trumpet while the supporting ideas offered by the remainder of the group assume more of a background position. These are just two of many ways that sound and silence can be shaped to influence how we feel as we engage with music.

Figure 4.3 Relational Balances Between Sound and Silence. *Source*: Created by Michele Kaschub and Janice P. Smith.

Another aspect of sound and silence is that of the quality of the sound. Choice of instruments as well as instrumental and vocal timbres change how music is experienced. Similarly, sounds may be bright/dark, warm/cool, staccato/legato, acoustic/electronic, and so on. Each of these sound qualities reflects a compositional choice that impacts how music is felt.

Tension and Release

Apprehension, excitement, and maybe a little nervousness often precede significant life events. Such events are often followed with a certain sense of relief. Music, too, can offer parallel experiences as tension grows and releases through the way sounds are shaped. Like unity and variety, nearly any aspect of music can be shaped to invite tension or provide release. A gradually expanding instrumentation, a steadily building dynamic, or a halting rhythmic figure embedded within a repetitive rhythmic framework can all produce tension and each can be countered to provide release in equal measure.

Stability and Instability

And finally, when life unfolds as expected, we feel stable and safe. But when there are surprises or challenges, we can begin to feel unsettled. Music, too, can have moments of stability or feel unsettled as it searches for firm ground. Music that extends too far into stability or instability is generally considered unpleasant. Stability quickly becomes tedious as there is nothing new to sustain attention and curiosity, while instability grows tiresome as the listener has to work too hard to stay engaged. Striking just the right balance between familiar and novel is a challenge pursued by composers in every genre.

Developing the Capacity of Musical Expressivity

Music teachers often focus on the elements of music (dynamics, form, harmony, melody, texture, tone color, and rhythm) as a means of making performances more expressive. Ironically, focusing exclusively on the elements in creating new music can lead to a lack of artistry. For example, asking a student to create a piece that contains a tempo change may allow the teacher to determine whether or not the student understands the concept of tempo and how to make such changes, but the inclusion of a tempo change in and of itself does not guarantee that the music will evoke a feelingful response.

Framing the compositional task in a manner that connects experience and feeling is a more effective approach. For example, students might be invited to create a piece of music that unfolds like a roller-coaster ride. As they think about what it is like to ride a roller coaster and consider how the ride feels from climbing aboard to the sense of survival at the finish, they are likely to explore form and changing tempo in a way that both reveals their conceptual understandings and leads to the creation of a work that features shifting balance between motion-stasis, tension-release, and perhaps other principles, too. In this way, the elements are not artificially strung together, but emerge as a natural part of the bigger picture, allowing expressive music to be made.

It is important to help students discover overarching feelingful intentions and musical expressivities as well as how those capacities present themselves within the work. The MUSTS can be applied at the level of the whole composition, to a single section of the work, or even across a phrase or measure. In creating the roller-coaster music described above, a composer might aim to create a composition that builds from a very stable, but tense beginning to a euphoric and relief-filled conclusion. Within that framework, there might be a section of the piece built on repetition at ever-increasing volume levels and higher speeds. The melody for that section might have a series of rising pitched motives that help create the feeling of tension. Thus tension, and most likely its subsequent release, occurs at the level of the whole composition, the section, and the phrase. Multi-level application may not suit all compositions, but students can be encouraged to think about the MUSTS to maximize the expressive potential of their music as is appropriate to their particular goals.

ARTISTIC CRAFTSMANSHIP

Artistic craftsmanship is the capacity to purposefully shape and organize sounds in a musically expressive manner that invites feelingful response. Composers need to familiarize themselves with a wide range of tools and master a considerable body of techniques to develop fluency in artistic craftsmanship. This takes time and careful guidance. When techniques are taught before feelingful intentions and musical expressivities have been considered, the compositional process becomes inauthentic. The music is disembodied from the composer and the learner is disengaged.

For example, middle school composers provided with a theory-focused lesson on range can create a piece that explores high and low pitches, but they may not be moved to use those pitches in an artistic manner. Conversely, if the young composers working on the theme-park-inspired pieces use a bass guitar to recall chugging up a roller-coaster mountain and an electric guitar to capture the squeal of the descent, the teacher can point out their musical decisions to introduce range and timbre as compositional tools. Approaching composition pedagogy in a manner that allows feelingful intention, musical expressivity, and artistic craftsmanship to be employed equally creates an opportunity for specific compositional techniques to be discovered in student work and made explicit in relation to each other. This promotes artistry and artistic thinking.

The phrase "tools and techniques of artistic craftsmanship" will appear throughout *Experiencing Music Composition*. "Tools" are those internal and external devices that influence and shape how young composers think. Internal tools include the musical imagination and inner hearing. Activities that encourage students to imagine sound and ways to manipulate those sounds foster the skill that allows composers to work without external sound sources. Similarly, systems that enable the imagination of sound through the use of symbols for pitch (solfeggio) or time (counting systems) also facilitate the composers' abilities to organize and shape sound in their minds.

External compositional tools include anything external to the composer that helps facilitate thinking. This may include instruments; computers; voices; smart devices; software, applications or web-based programs; lined and unlined manuscript paper; iconic, invented, or standardized notational systems; and recording devices. Tool choices change and evolve over time to suit the needs of the composer and the music being created. It is important that students experience a wide range of internal and external tools as they develop their personal vocabulary of composition.

"Technique" is the manner in which composers shape sound. It includes choices and decisions about how to use pitch, time, space, dynamics, form, instrumentation and orchestration, texture, and articulation. Students come to recognize technique through exposure. Activities such as singing, playing instruments, composing, improvising, and listening are all ways in which young composer might encounter compositional techniques. Once encountered, the teacher can name what has been experienced, offer a purposeful introduction, and engage students in experimentation that allows them to acquire the ability to use the technique in their own music-making. This sequence allows students to gain a multifaceted understanding of how and why composers use particular techniques in crafting their music.

Techniques and Études for Grades 6–8

While it is beyond the scope of this volume to address all the possible techniques that young composers may encounter or use in their work, the following material will provide possible avenues to pursue in fostering the development of artistic craftsmanship. The études suggested below range from initial explorations for first-time composers to more advanced challenges suitable for experienced eighth-grade students. Études serve to teach students about techniques outside of the act of composing. Composers benefit from instruction that introduces études once they have expressed an interest in particular technique or perceived a "need to know" moment in their own work.

The following labels are used to indicate the level of difficulty for each étude:

B. Beginner-level études are appropriate for middle school students with little to no previous composing experience.
I. Intermediate-level études are appropriate for middle school students with some previous experience.
A. Advanced-level études are appropriate for middle school students who are ready to tackle challenging and complex techniques.

Pitch

Composers should be encouraged to experiment and play with different modes, melodic constructs, and harmonies as a way to understand the impact of pitch on how music is experienced.

Mode

1. Create compositions using major, minor, pentatonic (B), chromatic, whole tone (I), invented (B), and other scales (I)
2. Use a single mode throughout a piece (B); use two modes in a single piece (I)

Melody

1. Invent a motive (B) and repeat or vary it throughout a piece (B)
2. Explore five different melodic shapes: pitches moving up, pitches moving down, smile (high–low–high), frown (low–high–low), and same (intervals remain static) (B)
3. Experiment with different types of motion—steps, skips, or leaps (B)
4. Compose a piece that is limited to a single type of motion, uses just two, or includes all three (I)
5. Reconstruct a stepwise melody to create a melody with larger intervals through intervallic expansion (I)
6. Decorate a melody with additional notes—ornamentation (B)
7. Remove notes from a melody—truncation (B)
8. Alter a melody by substituting different pitches or replacing pitches with rests (B)
9. Rewrite an existing melody backwards—retrograde (I)
10. Flip an existing melody upside down—inversion (I)
11. Create a new melody over an existing chord progression (I)

Harmony

1. Compose a repeating harmonic pattern to underpin or accompany a melody (B)
2. Create descant to fit an existing melody (I)

3. Add a countermelody to a previously composed melody (I)
4. Create a partner song for an existing song (I)
5. Explore harmonic boundaries by limiting works to single chords or using only tonic and dominant (B)
6. Explore chord progressions commonly found in specific genres, that is, Blues, 4-chord pop songs (I)

Time

Time is an organizing component of the musical experience used to measure the rate and duration of sounds. Musical time is revealed in the way beats are grouped metrically and subdivided to create rhythm. Composers also shape how we experience time through the use of tempo. Below are some ideas for exploring beat, meter, rhythm, and tempo.

Beat

1. Explore music with and without a steady beat (B)
2. Create music with strong and weak beats in predictable and unpredictable patterns (B)

Meter

1. Create music in simple and/or compound meters (B)
2. Convert a piece in simple meter to compound meter and vice versa (I)
3. Experiment with the subdivision of the meter (B)
4. Use multiple meters in a single work (I)

Rhythm

1. Create simple (B) and complex rhythms (A)
2. Create rhythmic ostinatos as accompaniment figures (B)
3. Explore rhythmic variation by adding notes within the beat (B)
4. Create syncopated rhythms (B)
5. Alter rhythms by replacing pitches with rests (B)
6. Layer rhythms to create percussion pieces (B)
7. Explore duration through augmentation or diminution of rhythmic note values (I)
8. Explore durational order reordering existing rhythms in retrograde (B)

Tempo

1. Explore how tempo changes can impact the mood or feelingful character of a work (B)
2. Incorporate multiple tempos within a single work (B)
3. Explore nuanced changes in tempo through use of accelerando, rallentando, and rubato (I)

Space

Composers do not always control the spaces in which their compositions will be heard. However, composers may specify the ways in which performers are intended to position themselves or their pieces and the ways that audiences should encounter them. Composers may give special thought to the locations in which their works will be performed, how performers will be physically placed within concert spaces, the mindset that performers and audiences might adopt when engaging with a work, and even storylines that imply other times and places. Some of these considerations are listed below.

Auditory Parameters

1. Create instructions that direct performers to multiple locations within a performance space to alter audience perceptions, that is, orchestra on stage, small groups of instrumentalists off stage or situated behind the audience (I)
2. Explore panning (side to side) frequencies (high to low), and intensity (close physical proximity to distant horizon) when positioning sounds to be played through speakers (B)

Conceptual Spaces

1. Specify a performance space to capitalize on connotations that people bring to the space, that is, the rowdiness of a school gymnasium versus the reverence of a memorial site (B)
2. Write program notes that invoke a particular time, space, or set of conditions to frame a musical work or the audiences' experience of the work (I)

Performance Environment

1. Specify the setup for a concert environment: performers on stage and listeners in audience (B)
2. Create instructions that require a participatory environment in which performers and listeners intermingle so that audience is part of the performance (B)
3. Compose a work for a virtual environment. Performers and audience will connect virtually in real-time or asynchronously (I)
4. Create a work to be experienced through earbuds in an individual environment where specifications relate to panning (B)

Temporal Space

1. Create an "extra-temporal" timeline through the use of program notes or lyrics that describe another time/space and seek to transport the audience into that world (B)

Dynamics

Dynamic levels within a work mark important changes in intensity and do not refer to decibel levels (volume). Changes in dynamics may be achieved in several different ways and influence how music is shaped by performers and experienced by listeners. Composers can manipulate dynamics by altering intensity, relationship, and balance.

Intensity

1. Create varying degrees of intensity by changing written/performed dynamic levels (B)
2. Explore changes in instrumentation: the more instruments, voices, or other sound sources contributing to a soundscape, the greater the intensity of the music (B)
3. Use different combinations of instruments, voices, or other sound sources to capitalize on natural acoustic properties, that is, children's voices produce sound waves that travel differently than do the sound waves generated by a quartet of tubas (B)

Relational

1. Offer sudden changes in character of the music through use of *subito* dynamics, that is, *sfz—subito forzando*, "suddenly with force" (B)
2. Create gradual changes in character of the music through use of *crescendo* and *decrescendo*. (B)

Balance and Blend

1. Set dynamic levels for different sections of a piece (B)
2. Specify different dynamic levels for each instrument to increase or decrease presence within texture (I)

Form

Musical form refers to the overall architecture of musical sounds. Organization levels can be viewed from large structures (i.e., symphonies), to mid-level components (i.e., the "A" section), or smaller structures (i.e., phrases). The formal constructs below are listed from smallest to largest in scope.

Motive

1. Create a melodic motive of at least four pitches and then explore the ways it may be varied by altering only the rhythm (B)
2. Explore how the impact of a rhythm is altered when pitches are added—within a single pitch class, close intervals, distant intervals, etc. (B)

Phrase

1. Extend a motive into a phrase through the use of sequence, motivic variation, or other elongation techniques (I)
2. Transform a motive into an imitative gesture by passing it between two instruments or voices (B)
3. Alter melodic contours and supporting harmonies to lengthen or shorten phrases (I)
4. Experiment with varying the ending of the phrase to create different feelings—question, answer, uncertainty, surprise, and so on. (I)

Period

1. Experiment with half cadences and cadential elisions as ways of joining phrases to build periods (I)

Section

1. Construct different formal structures such AB, ABA, AAB, ABB, rondo, blues, 32-bar song, and other forms (I)

Movement

1. Compose several shorter works with some unifying aspect that allows them to be grouped together into a longer work (I)

Full Work

1. Consider the classification of the work identifying the specific genre, particular style, or performance practice (I)
2. Draw connections between multiple works (I)

Instrumentation and Orchestration

Instrumentation is the choice of particular sounds or combination of sounds while orchestration refers to the way the instruments are used to create particular moods. Once a composer has selected instruments, orchestration may be more specifically tailored to invite particular affective response.

Sound Sources

1. Select instruments, voices, or other sound sources to be used in music composition and explain why each was chosen for inclusion (B)
2. Compose pieces for solo instrument, voice, or other sound source to focus on its particular abilities and idiomatic tendencies (I)

Timbre

1. Explore the different qualities of an individual instrument, voice, or other sound source in terms of character and quality (I)
2. Combine two or more instruments, voices, or other sound sources to explore the interrelationships between different characters and qualities of sound (B)
3. Create pieces that use instruments from a single family—woodwind, brass, string, percussion, keyboard, electronic, and so on. (I)
4. Compose a work that juxtapositions instruments from two or more different families (I)

Range

1. Experiment with the full range of pitches (highest to lowest) available for a single or combination of instruments, voices, or other sound sources to determine the impact of outer margins versus center (I)

Register

1. Create music that capitalizes on the tone quality of a particular instrument, voice, or other sound source. (I)
2. Explore how different instruments, voices, or sound sources take on different qualities in different registers and how this influences combinations of instruments, voices, or other sound sources. (I)

Tessitura

1. Compose music within a range of pitches that are appropriate—easy to produce and pleasant-sounding—to specific instruments, voices, or other sound sources (I)
2. Purposefully create music with pitches that are within the capacity but beyond the "comfort zone" of specific instruments, voices, or other sound sources (I)

Texture

Texture refers layers of sound. Texture may include how many independent and dependent musical lines are present, how many instruments or voices are in use, how many sounds are unfolding simultaneously, and the relative presence or absence of particular sounds in the piece at any given moment. Below are a few activities that explore different types of texture.

Monophonic

1. Create unaccompanied melodies for solo and unison parts (B)
2. Compose pieces that contrast unison sections with other textures. (B)

Biphonic

1. Create works with two distinct parts: one line is melodic, the other is simpler and serves as accompaniment. (B)

Homophonic Movement

1. Create works with two or more parts moving in identical rhythm, but with different pitches to imply chordal harmony (I)
2. Use an existing harmonic progression to create a new work (I)
3. Create works for solo instruments with simple chordal accompaniment (I)

Polyphonic Movement

1. Create rounds and canons (B)
2. Write countermelodies and descants to fit existing songs or original melodies (I)
3. Explore counterpoint by creating intertwining melodies with and without accompaniment (A)

Articulation

Articulation refers to the way that musical sounds start and end. The use of specific attack and release types can contribute to the distinctive character of the musical style.

Attack

1. Experiment with different ways of producing a sound, that is, staccato, accent, tenuto, marcato, double or triple tonguing, flutter tongue, pizzicato, up-bow, down-bow, pluck, slap, hard versus soft mallets, and so on. (B)

Release

1. Explore different ways of ending sounds, that is, arco, pizzacato, damped, fade out, and so on. (B)

Developing the Capacity of Artistic Craftsmanship

Any of the preceding techniques of artistic craftsmanship can be taught as the need arises within the context of a composer's own work or as part of a class focusing on a specific tool or technique. In class settings, short lessons on new concepts or tools are often an effective way of moving a group of middle school composers forward to new possibilities. Such introductions should always focus on how the resulting music sounds. The students' own performance or recordings can be used to illustrate new compositional ideas and to bring into discussion the consideration of how such ideas can be used to achieve expressive ends. Students also can be invited to suggest or shown how such ideas might be notated in invented, iconographic, or traditional notation. By developing ear and eye together, students expand their compositional palette.

FINAL THOUGHTS

The capacities of feelingful intention, musical expressivity, and artistic craftsmanship may be discussed at nearly any point in the compositional process. The key point is that each must be brought into the conscious thought of young musicians in order for them to develop their ideas and to grow as composers. The capacities help students move beyond the "fortuitous accident" stage where they occasionally and unintentionally generate a satisfying musical idea to the point where they create by design. When students consider and deliberately use MUSTS in their work, the tools and techniques they use serve as the sonic connection between lived experience and feeling. Those feelingful relationships often free young composers to think more expressively about music composition so that they may create artistic and personally meaningful work.

Chapter 5

Using *Sketchpages*

GUIDING THE JOURNEY

Have you ever taken a walk in an unfamiliar place and wondered if you would ever find your way? Composers often experience a similar degree of concern as they attempt to travel from musical idea to musical work. Within *Experiencing Music Composition*, compositional paths are illuminated through the use of *Sketchpages*—student guides that combine open doodle space, thinking prompts, and composer sketchbooks.

Sketchpages accompany every lesson in this volume. They are designed to help students explore their musical ideas as they consider the connections between feelingful intention, musical expressivity, and artistic craftsmanship. The pages serve as inspirational spaces where students jot ideas during or between composing sessions. These ideas become points of reference, helping students monitor their progress from initial imaginings through the final product. *Sketchpages* may be added to or revised by students as their compositional journey unfolds. Most importantly, as open documents, the use of *Sketchpages* can remove the pressure to arrive quickly at a finished piece.

The main purpose of a *Sketchpage* is to provide a practical tool that composers can use to explore and develop the potential of their musical ideas. *Sketchpages* can be particularly helpful when teachers and students discuss musical ideas that primarily exist in the student's imagination. As a visual representation of key compositional ideas and relationships, *Sketchpage*s allow composers to pursue the processes suited to their own preferred working styles.

Each *Sketchpage* or collection of *Sketchpages* features prompts that correspond to each of the compositional capacities. This allows teachers and students to begin with any capacity and build toward the remaining two capacities. Whether composers are working with images, words, sound recording apps, or using invented or traditional notation, *Sketchpages* can be used to capture compositional ideas ranging from motives to fully articulated, large-scale works. This helps composers manage the details of music-making in a productive manner.

Every project in this collection can be tailored to match the notational skill level of middle school composers. These reproducible guides can be copied and distributed to students or downloaded from the companion website for use by students. In addition to these guides, there are three different types of notation paper which can be copied and placed where student may simply collect the sheet they need as they work. The invented notation page is primarily white space. The two transitions sheets have both white space for invented notation and staff paper to use as students learn to notate their ideas. The transition sheets are designed so that students may choose to notate ideas independently or to align music event in time. The final sheet is staff paper and suited to students who are comfortable with notating their ideas in the traditional manner.

INTRODUCING *SKETCHPAGES* TO MIDDLE SCHOOL COMPOSERS

The best way to introduce the use of *Sketchpages* to composers is to facilitate a teacher-guided whole-class composition activity. Whole-group activities begin with the teacher projecting the *Sketchpage*, which can be found at https://rowman.com/ISBN/9781475864618/Experiencing-Music-Composition-in-Middle-School-General-Music, so that all students can see it and work on it together. The teacher describes the composition task and invites students to discuss each of the guiding questions or prompts while noting student ideas and answers on the *Sketchpage*. With a little guidance, students should be able to work through a *Sketchpage* with a partner, in a small group, and eventually, by themselves.

When students first begin to use *Sketchpages*, they are likely to create simple one-to-one-to-one relationships in which they identify a single feelingful intention fulfilled through one of the principle pairs (MUSTS) and crafted through the use of a single technique.

Figure 5.1 "Duetto"—A Student Composition. *Source*: Created by Michele Kaschub and Janice P. Smith.

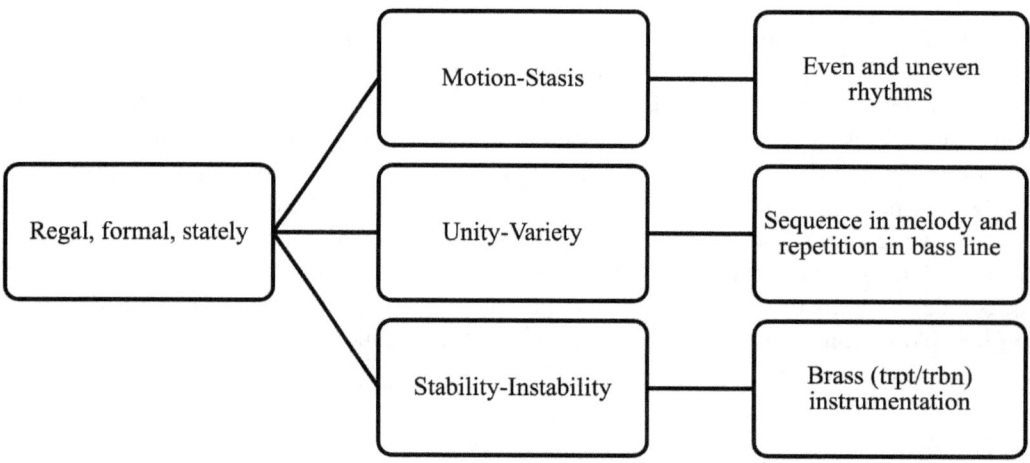

Figure 5.2 Student Illustration of Relationship between Capacities in "Duetto." *Source*: Created by Michele Kaschub and Janice P. Smith.

Feelingful Intention	Musical Expressivity	Artistic Craftsmanship
Regal, formal stately	(trumpet) (trombone) Motion---Δ----------------------Δ---Stasis Unity---Δ--------------------------Variety Sound---Δ--------------------------Silence Tension-------------Δ-------------Release Stability--Δ---------------------Instability	• Trombone uses quarter notes to create motion and stability • Trumpet uses uneven rhythms to create forward motion in contrast with even rhythm of trombone • Unity – same key and character throughout • Tension/release – measure 4, C# in trumpet needs/finds resolution • Stable – as expected for fanfare

Figure 5.3 **Student Explanation of Capacity Connections.** *Source*: Created by Michele Kaschub and Janice P. Smith.

Figure 5.1 is a duet created by two third-year instrumentalists. Figure 5.2 illustrates the connections that the composers made between feelingful intentions, musical expressivities, and artistic craftsmanship, while figure 5.3 documents how the composers explained the connections between the capacities.

As student compositions become increasingly multifaceted, graphic representations of their works reveal an ever-expanding array of connections. Figure 5.4 shows a very simple one-to-one-to-one (one feelingful intention

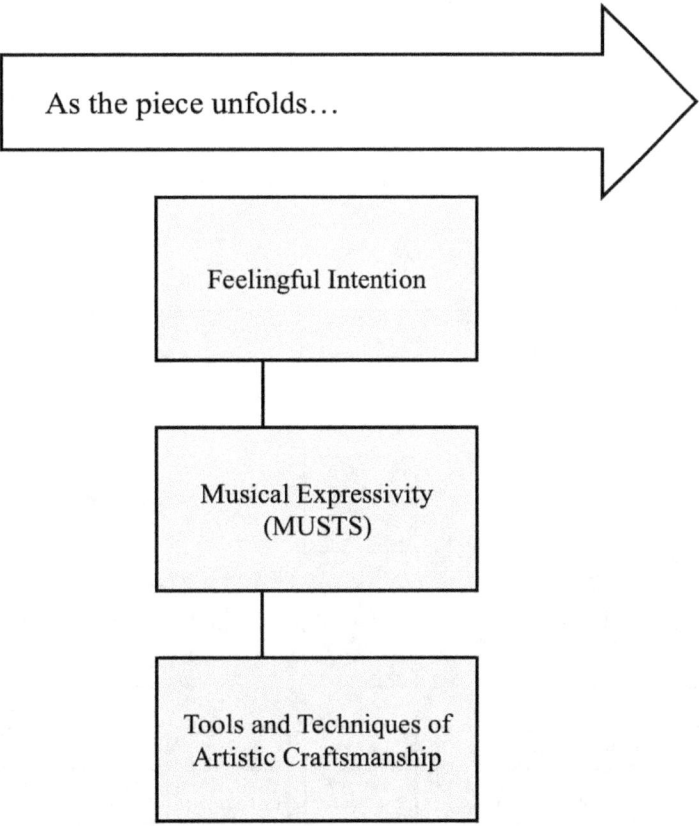

Figure 5.4 **Simple 1-1-1 Relationship of Capacities.** *Source*: Created by Michele Kaschub and Janice P. Smith.

to one musical expressivity to one tool or technique of artistic craftsmanship) relationship of composer thought. Figure 5.5 shows a diagram of intermediate complexity where a single feelingful intention is achieved through the activation of two musical expressivities each achieved through the use of single compositional technique. For example, if a composer is working with "anticipation" as the identified feelingful intention, the composer might employ unity and variety through the use of a rhythmic ostinato built of three half-notes (unity) and two quarter notes (variety) while simultaneously building tension through the use of an elongated crescendo. Unity/variety and tension/release are the dominant musical expressivities that connect the rhythmic and dynamic techniques to the sense of anticipation.

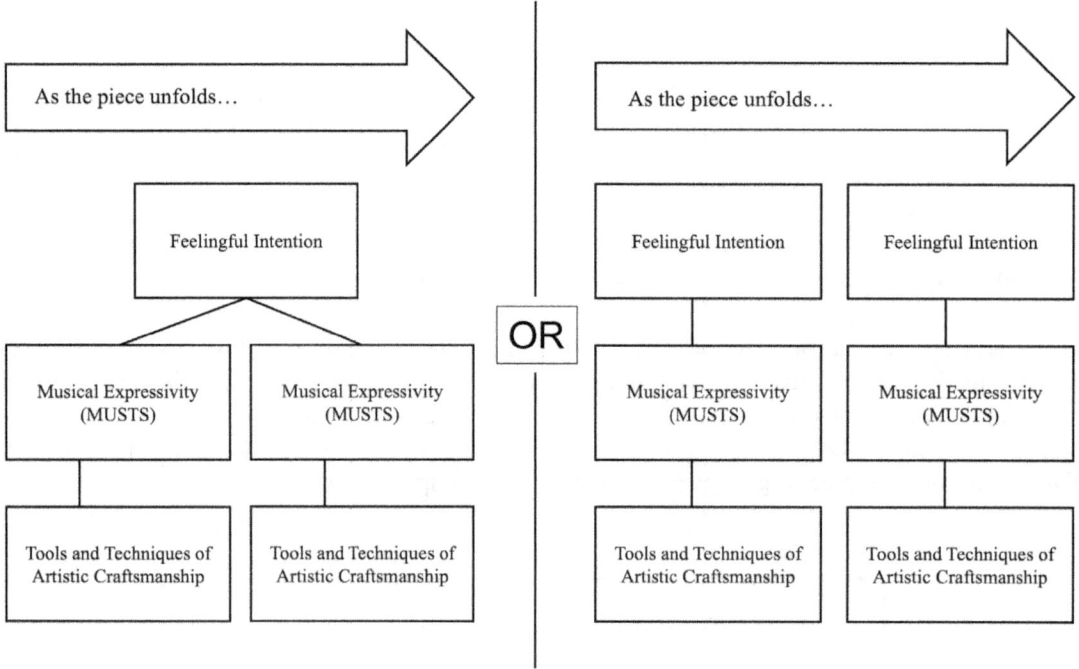

Figure 5.5 Graphic Representations of Intermediate Relationship Complexity among Capacities. *Source*: Created by Michele Kaschub and Janice P. Smith.

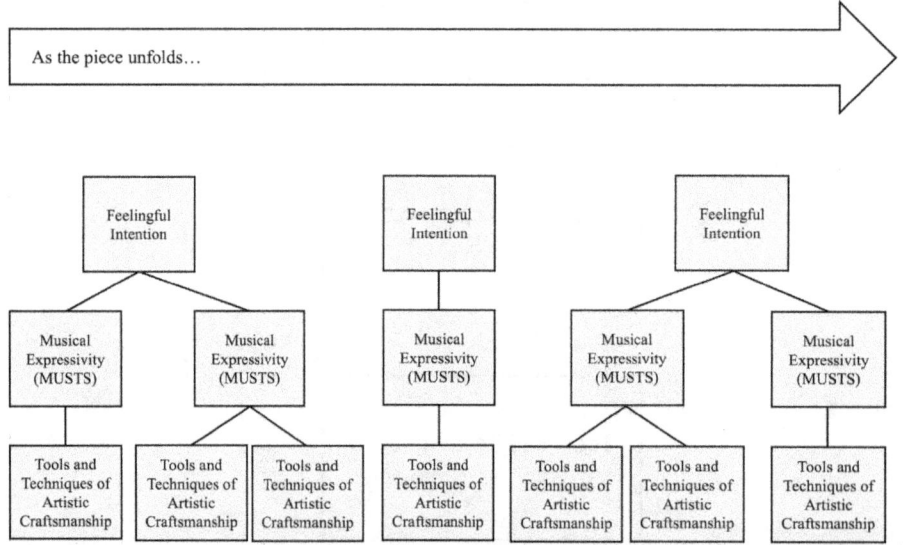

Figure 5.6 Complex Graphic Organizer Representing Highly Complex Relationship among Capacities. *Source*: Created by Michele Kaschub and Janice P. Smith.

Figure 5.6 reveals the complex interconnections of a much more advanced work in which the feelingful intention changes as the piece unfolds and calls upon additional expressivities and tools of craftsmanship to be used. Regardless of how simple or complex the connections between capacities may be, the key role that *Sketchpages* fulfill is the facilitation of learning.

SKETCHPAGES AS MULTITASKERS

Sketchpages can fill many roles as teachers and students work together. Teachers can use *Sketchpages* to develop a better understanding of each composer's needs as students use the graphic organizers to help them move musical ideas from their imaginations into the world.

Teachers can use *Sketchpages* to:

1. facilitate the development of each student's compositional capacities.
2. encourage the development of critical and creative thinking skills as students imagine, execute, and reflect on their compositional ideas.
3. gain a better understanding of each student's compositional processes.
4. provide meaningful and pointed feedback reflective of the student's compositional goals.
5. assess, in collaboration with the student, the student's work.

Students can use *Sketchpages* to:

1. remember key ideas and concepts essential to their feelingful intent.
2. understand the relationship between feelingful intent, musical expressivities (MUSTS), and the tools of artistic craftsmanship.
3. apply their knowledge and skills to develop and extend initial ideas and conceptions.
4. analyze problems and consider multiple solutions to a broad range of compositional challenges.
5. evaluate a product vision for solo, partnered, small group or large group work.
6. isolate specific compositional challenges.
7. create expressive compositions that invite performers and audiences to meaningfully engage with music.

Section 3

CREATIVE POSITIVE COMPOSITIONAL EXPERIENCES

Chapter 6

Composition Requires a Different Kind of Teaching

*The music that middle school composers create represents a deeply
personal investment and may reveal an unguarded sharing of feelings and emotions.
This creates a potentially fragile learning environment.
Teachers must make every effort to establish and maintain learning spaces
that are supportive and encouraging so that every student feels safe
as music is shared and feedback is given.*

Teaching composition is different from teaching performance or leading listening lessons. Making something new is a little more creative and a little more chaotic than reproducing or describing something that already exists. When teaching composition as we advocate in the *Experiencing Music Composition* approach, the end product is not known when the lesson begins.

In both listening and performance lessons, the teacher knows and often controls what the end result will be. The teacher usually determines how pieces are supposed to sound and identifies the knowledge that students should acquire. In composition classes, the lack of a preconceived product requires teachers to trust themselves and their students. They are engaging in a process where learning and its products will naturally emerge over time.

The *Experiencing Music Composition* approach has its foundations in discovery learning and in the constructivist approach to learning. Springing from the work of Jerome Bruner,[1] Jean Piaget,[2] and John Dewey,[3] the central tenet of the approach involves engaging students in activities that pose authentic challenges within a specific domain. The students draw on their own experiences and prior knowledge as they consider how to address these challenges. Because students take the lead in defining problems, testing solutions and making decisions about which actions to pursue, they become strongly invested in the learning process. While this investment is integral to the achievement of compositional success, it is not the only component. The manner in which teachers approach tasks also greatly influences student learning.

Like their students, most teachers know much more about music composition than they think they do. Teachers know what makes a sing-able melody, how to vary a motive, and how changing tone colors may alter the character of a musical idea. Creating lists of techniques and specifying how they should be applied may enable the crafting of a product, but it does so at the cost of student ownership and autonomy. For individual artistry, creativity, and personal growth to emerge from their work, student ownership and autonomy are a necessary component of composition experiences. Here are two teaching scenarios that illustrate why the teacher's approach matters.

SCENARIO 1: MX. ADDO'S FIRST SONGWRITING PROJECT

Mx. Addo's students are scheduled to present their projects today. Each team of students has been asked to create an original folk song that demonstrates a verse-refrain form. Students have discussed how verse-refrain songs can be organized and learned how to play D, G, and A chords on the guitar. They have listened to a few folksongs that use the I-IV-V-I chord progression. Mx. Addo also has given each team a checklist to serve as a guide for making sure that these requirements are fulfilled.

- Work in groups of two to three people
- Create two verses
- Create a refrain
- Use D, G, and A chords
- Start and end on I chord (D)
- Be ready to perform your song for the class

As the performances take place, Mx. Addo proudly notices that each team has successfully used the chord progression and all have written two verses and a refrain. Yet, the pieces seem flat. Students have created lyrics about topics that are important in their daily lives—lost homework, uncooperative lockers, lost gym clothes, and the like—but something is missing. The songs are not very engaging and the students seem to be just going through the motions.

SCENARIO 2: MX. ADDO'S REVISED FOLK SONG PROJECT

Mx. Addo's students have been listening to and singing folk songs from several different countries. They have discussed the similarities and differences between the songs in terms of lyrics, basic harmonies, and social function. Believing that the students grasp the idea of what a folk song is and how they are created and shared, Mx. Addo introduces a folk song composing project:

We have sung songs from the American Southwest, Canada, Germany, the Czech Republic, South Korea, the Democratic Republic of the Congo, and Jamaica. Each of these songs has told a story from the point of view of a particular person in a particular place at a particular time. Today, we are going to begin to write our own songs. I have given each of you a guide sheet which addresses four key concerns:

1. *Who do I represent in this song?*
2. *Where is this story taking place? Why?*
3. *What am I doing there? Why does it matter?*
4. *What is special about me/doing this thing/at this time/in this place?*

There are many possible answers to these questions. Put your imagination to work and tell a story that invites us, your audience, to understand your point of view in a new way.

Once you have a story idea in mind, answer these questions for each verse and/or refrain as you make up your song:

1. *What do I want the audience to feel (feelingful intention) as they hear my song?*
2. *Which of the musical expressivities (MUSTS) will most influence the experience of the audience during this verse/refrain?*
3. *Which tools and techniques of artistic craftsmanship can I use to convey my story?*

Mx. Addo then reminded the students of the chords they knew how to play on the guitar and suggested that additional chords could be shown to them if they needed some other options to capture the feelingful intention of their songs.

After a few class sessions, Mx. Addo's students were finished composing and rehearsing their pieces. The students arranged chairs in a semi-circle with place at the top for the performers to sit. As each team took the class stage and sang through their folksong, Mx. Addo noted not only the use of D-G-A chords, but also a handful of E-minors and even a B-minor substitution that added a particularly reminiscent touch. Some of the songwriters sought to create contrasting moods between their verses and refrains. Nearly all had explored dynamics and boastful refrains. Gentle fades marked a handful of pieces. Moreover, as students reflected on their work, the discussion revealed a growing grasp of music's potential to express more than just the words of the song.

Process, and student agency within that process, matter greatly in compositional work. Students need to be given enough guidance to feel secure and sufficient freedom to explore their own artistic ideas. Finding this balance requires identifying students' musical skills as well as their personal management skills as they pertain to organization and self-directed learning. When students feel that they know what they are supposed to do in a broad sense but are given permission to work out the finer details themselves, they tend to be more engaged and motivated than students whose every step and task is tightly controlled.

WORKING WITH "IN-PROCESS" COMPOSERS

Sometimes it is difficult to trust that students will come up with ideas. However, the process of composing is quite similar to the experiences young people have when they pursue creative writing. Given time and a little encouragement, they eventually find an idea and get underway. One particular challenge in music composition is that students often have musical ideas in their heads that they cannot articulate or perform. This is where the teacher can help by prompting students to think critically about what they are imagining.

Asking questions that evoke imaginative responses often helps students take a step toward getting started or advancing a germinal idea. For example, when students are creating a piece for their instruments, ask them to close their eyes and imagine themselves performing on stage while an audience sits and listens. Wait a few seconds and then add that everyone claps enthusiastically when the performance has ended. Ask the student to describe the piece they imagined.[4] Jot these thoughts down for the student or have them add them to their *Sketchpage*.

Another example of evoking imagination might be: "Imagine that the creator of 'Crash Course,' a new video series for social media offering how-to guidance on a variety of outlandish topics, has asked you to score their 10-minute episodes. The show has a host who travels to various locals to interview and work alongside experts on the topic of each 'crash course.' What kind of music might match the expectations of the viewer? How will the theme anchor/identify the show? How will you determine how to vary the music of each episode to reflect its particular topic?"

The technique of using questions to prompt student action requires knowledge of the student and what might be blocking his or her creativity. Some students will simply state what their problem is, while others may have a hard time figuring it how to name it or describe it. Some students have a very clear idea of what they want their music to sound like, but cannot figure out how to make (or notate) the sounds. Other students are simply shy, or hesitant to share their ideas. While these situations can be frustrating for student and teacher alike, they are temporary and will resolve with practice and supportive guidance. Let's consider two key points in the process when students are likely to get stuck and ask for help: idea generation and idea development/extension.

Idea Generation

Students often wonder where to begin their pieces. There is no correct answer for this question. The *Sketchpages* provided with each lesson present multiple entry points to each project. It is important to remember that every composer will find an individual entry point of comfort. For some composers, this will be a feeling or mood. Other composers may select an instrument or quickly discover a melodic or rhythmic fragment that sets the stage for the use of specific compositional techniques. Regardless of where and how the process starts, encourage students to think about the connections among all three capacities to enhance the overall quality of their work.

Idea Development or Expansion

Once composers have a work-in-progress, they may come to the teacher with questions about how a particular idea might evolve, or more directly, to ask what should come next. *Be very careful in offering a response.* It is easy to share solutions that are obvious to you as a "quick fix." It is more beneficial to the student to figure out the answer to the question that they have posed for themselves. When possible, ask, don't tell.

Begin by asking to hear the piece and be prepared to listen more than once. Repeated listenings can be facilitated by saying, "I'm hearing a lot in this piece. May I hear it again so that I can get a better idea of what you are trying to do?" Once you have a clearer sense of what has been created, discuss the work with the composer using the following questions as is appropriate:

1. What should I know about your piece?
2. Where did you begin?
3. Was there a feeling, a particular MUSTS pair that was appealing, or a technique that you are trying to use?
4. How are you trying to capture that feeling?
5. What are you doing to feature [insert MUSTS pair named by the student]?
6. How does the starting point capacity connect to the other capacities?
7. Is there something specific that you are trying to do?
8. What have you tried in an attempt to solve the current challenge?
9. Are there other things you might try?
10. Have you considered the idea that this music might be the middle or end of your piece rather than the beginning? Just because you create something first, it doesn't have to be the beginning. (Adapt to whatever location a student might be stuck in their work.)
11. Have you listened to any other composers who have worked with this genre, form, instrumentation, etc.? What solutions did they use?
12. Would you like me to offer a few options for you to try to see if they help you find what you are after?

As much as is possible, follow the student's lead in the discussion. Save the offer of presenting options as a final resort for times when students are truly at a loss for what to do. When presenting options, offer at least three and make sure that composers know that they do not have to use any of the presented options. The options are simply shared in hopes of spurring further exploration and idea trials to prompt student thinking.

ANCHORING KNOWLEDGE, INVITING INSPIRATION

Another way to help students gain independence within the compositional process is to make a wide variety of resources available to them. Brief playlists organized by historical period, genre, style, compositional techniques or other categorizations can provide auditory inspiration to composers facing specific challenges. Likewise, visual quick reference tools can serve to remind students of what they know or allow them to make important connections that further their work.

One such visual reference tool is the "Anchor Chart." These posters can be created from student observations of how music works. As students listen to music, sing songs, or play instruments, they can be invited to notice and discuss compositional gestures. The techniques that they observe can then be recorded on posters, webpages or other easily accessed locations, "anchoring" what has been learned for students to reference as they carry out their own compositional work. Consider creating charts that list feelingful intentions, document ways that composers use each of the MUSTS pairs, or list specific compositional techniques that the students have mastered or are currently exploring within their work.

While teachers can make and post resource charts, student-created charts constitute the most powerful learning tools because students feel a personal investment in the information represented. Each chart will be unique as it reflects what the students of a particular compositional community have discovered and analyzed together. Similarly, anchor charts do not have a set format. Rather, each chart evolves as teachers and students work together to document what they have discovered about a topic, tool, or idea. A quick Internet search for "music anchor chart" turns up a vast array of designs. Anchor charts may be focused on any capacity, may be organized by the MUSTS (musical expressivities), or include definitions of key concepts, lists of ideas, or steps in process. The requirement common to all anchor charts is that they must be useful to the students who will use them. An example of a completed anchor chart is shown in figure 6.1.

Techniques for Creating Unity–Variety	
Unity	**Variety**
Repeat a melodic motive within or between formal units	Expand intervals (through use of skip and leap) within the melodic motive after the motive has been established in the piece (also impacts stability)
Establish a repeating harmonic pattern (series of chords)	Use substitution chords to alter change pattern and alter character
Use a single meter	Alternate between duple and triple meters
Use minimal dynamic contrast within formal units (i.e., a single phrase)	Explore dramatic dynamic contrasts within and between formal units

Figure 6.1 Anchor Chart for Unity-Variety. *Source*: Created by Michele Kaschub and Janice P. Smith.

GUIDELINES FOR SHARING COMPOSITIONS—GIVING AND RECEIVING FEEDBACK

Sharing compositions for feedback allows students the opportunity to improve their work while it is still in progress. It gives them direct insight as to how a particular audience may react and allows them to critically reflect on their own work and the works of others. As composers share music with each other, they discover new musical ideas, different ways of achieving particular outcomes and compositional techniques that may be of use to them in the moment or in the future.

In addition to musical skills, middle school composers also develop enhanced communication skills as they speak about their work and offer praise and critique on the work of their peers. As their experiences with composition and presentation grow, they gain confidence in their ability to meet and describe their intentions. They become increasingly able to describe their working processes and they recognize the ongoing development of their compositional capacities. To foster this growth, teachers must create and maintain an environment that allows students to feel safe in sharing work that is often highly personal. The best way to do this is through a direct partnership with students.

Setting Expectations and Creating Guidelines

Before students can offer feedback on the compositions of their peers, they need an opportunity to think about how they will feel as they receive comments. Teachers can invite students to imagine sharing a composition with their classmates and prompt them to think about type of feedback that they would hope to receive. Students should also consider how they would like comments made.

Begin with a composition model created by the teacher or a student who is not in the class. Be sure to keep the composer anonymous and if using a student work, do so only with the permission of the composer. Have students listen to this piece and then practice offering praise and constructive feedback. Use the statements made by the students as examples to put together a list of guidelines, such as those shown in figure 6.2, to help students provide useful feedback in a pleasant and supportive manner.

> - Be kind and give the type of feedback that you would hope to receive.
> - Offer praise.
> - Critique the composition; do not criticize the composer (performer).
> - Be specific in your feedback so that the composer knows exactly what you are talking about.
> - Talk about what the composer asked listeners to comment on.
> - Speak from your own perspective using phrases such as:
>   - I think_____worked for me because_____.
>   - The use of_____made me feel_____.
>   - As I listened to your piece, I learned that_____.
>   - I'm wondering if you tried_____? I ask because_____.
>   - Maybe you could try_____because it_____.
>   - I'm curious about_____. Can you tell us why_____?

Figure 6.2 Tips for Composers Offering Feedback. *Source*: Created by Michele Kaschub and Janice P. Smith.

It is also important for composers to think about how they will accept feedback. It can be difficult to listen to what others have to say about work that you are deeply connected to and perhaps quite proud of. However, middle school composers benefit from experiences that require them to gain some objective distance from their music so that they can thoughtfully evaluate what is working and what may need further work. Figure 6.3 outlines a few thoughts that composers should keep in mind as they listen to feedback.

> - Listen. Just listen. Do not attempt to justify your approach. Simply pay attention to how others are reacting and responding to your work so that you can decide if you wish to change anything or continue on the path you have pursued so far.
> - Be open to ideas that don't immediately make sense to you. New listeners hear differently than you do.
> - Suggestions are only suggestions. You do not have to change your music to address every suggestion that is offered.
> - Listen to praise. It highlights your best work and points out the skills that you have and can use to improve your piece.

Figure 6.3 Tips for Composers Receiving Feedback. *Source*: Created by Michele Kaschub and Janice P. Smith.

Composers' Circles

Composers' Circles are gatherings of composers, teachers, performers, and others who may provide useful feedback on compositions-in-progress or completed works. Composers' Circles can be used in face-to-face and online environments. They may involve whole classes when composition projects have been completed in small groups, but may also be limited in size with just three to five composers who listen to each other's work and offer constructive commentary. If students are working in an online environment, it may be beneficial for students to record acoustic performances and share audio or video recordings. This will reduce issues arising from latency.

It is important that teachers facilitate initial Composers' Circles so that students learn how to fill the roles of presenter and responder. Circles typically begin with a composer, or group of composers, introducing a piece. The composer should be encouraged to share any information that may be relevant to the listeners. This may include information about inspiration, feelingful intentions, musical expressivities, techniques being used, or problems that the composer is seeking to address. Figure 6.4 shows some statements that may help young composers introduce their work.

- The piece that I am working on is called _____.
- I am trying to create the feeling of _____.
- I have used (M.U.S.T.S) to try to invite a feeling of _____.
- The first musical idea that I tried _____.
- I have tried using (technique) _____ to _____, but I am finding that _____.
- I know I need to work on _____.
- I am hoping that someone might have a suggestion for how I could _____.
- I am open to any reaction.
- Please tell me *what* you think works and *why* you think it works for you.

Figure 6.4 Following the Composer's Lead. *Source*: Created by Michele Kaschub and Janice P. Smith.

Once the introduction has been given and the audience has heard the work, the teacher should encourage students to offer constructive criticisms. It is helpful to invite praise and criticism in balance—two praise comments to each comment of constructive criticism. As students become comfortable with this process and gain confidence as composers, the balance of comments may be adjusted to suit the needs of each composer as is shown in the written comment form of figure 6.5.

	Critic 1:	Critic 2:	Critic 3:
Bravo!			
Bravo!			
An idea to consider			
An idea to consider			
What, if any, ideas for revision did you take from this feedback?			

Composer Feedback
Title: _____
Composer(s): _____

Figure 6.5 Composer Feedback Guide. *Source*: Created by Michele Kaschub and Janice P. Smith with images from iStock/Credit: Sudowoodo and kotoffei.

Working with Reluctant Sharers

Composers who do not receive feedback on their work are unlikely to further develop their compositional capacities. Therefore, it is important to find ways to provide feedback to reluctant sharers as soon as possible. Unfortunately, some middle school composers may be very reluctant to share what they have created. They may not even want to share their composition with friends or the teacher. In such cases, it is important to respect the young composer's reluctance while continuing to show interest in what they are doing.

Some students will agree to participate in one-on-one conferences, either with the teacher or a friend within the class. Others will be comfortable with recording their compositions so that the teacher can listen to them apart from the student with feedback taking written form. In this situation, written feedback in early interactions must offer valid praise with only a few minor criticisms. This will help students overcome the fear of criticism while allowing some productive feedback to be given.

As trust grows, students can be gently led into greater participation in the Composers' Circle. Interaction should begin with reluctant sharers being invited to offer praise and then suggestions, but not expected to share their work. By participating in this way, their confidence may grow and they may begin to feel emotionally safe within the group. Once trust has been established and developed, reluctant sharers may become more willing to present their music for feedback.

Putting Feedback to Good Use

The feedback that middle school composers receive from the teacher or peers within the Composer's Circle holds varying potential. Composers often put the ideas presented to them to immediate use if they are working on a composition that is still in progress but are far less likely to apply suggestions to a finished work.

Encouraging students to revise work that they consider completed requires a cautious approach. Composers who have completed a work on a piece may consider themselves finished with it and ready to move on to the next thing. However, skipping from project to project at this point may hinder the development of critical analysis and reflection skills necessary for students to objectively evaluate their own work. Mentors can make suggestions like "I think there is potential for this to be a longer piece. Do you think there might be another part to it?" or "You have created a [descriptive word capturing the composer's feelingful intention] song. I wonder if it might be the chorus of a longer piece?" While middle school composers might entertain these questions, they may not agree or wish to start a new work. It is important to respect their developmental stage while continuing to find ways to introduce revision as part of the compositional process. Students may be more open to suggestions for revisions if those suggestions further their own artistic intentions.

Reflecting After the Performance

As students share the final versions of their pieces, teachers should facilitate questioning that reveals multiple feelingful intentions or the depth to which a single or a few different feelings have been utilized, each of the musical expressivities (motion-stasis, unity-variety, sound-silence, tension-release, and stability-instability) in prominent and secondary/supporting roles, and the tools and techniques of artistic craftsmanship. Multiple aspects of each of the capacities unfold in every piece. Taking time to identify specific capacities and discuss how they work reveals music's complex constructions and potentials for expressive artistry.

Moreover, some students will discover new things about their own compositions as they describe them and as they hear the observations made by those who have listened to their work. Other students will recognize their own techniques and processes only when they hear similar ones described by their peers. Allowing the processes of composition to be experienced directly, observed, and overtly discussed presents myriad entry points for middle school composers to learn more about themselves and the art of composition. The *Critical Reflections Guide* shown in figure 6.6 and found in the appendix can be used with each project in this volume to promote individual thinking and to prompt group discussion.

Critical Reflection Guide

Composition Title:_____ Name:_____

What did I learn from this composition project?

FI-ME-AC Connections

I/We used *(an element or tool of Artistic Craftsmanship)*
to invite the perception of *(Musical Expressivity/single M.U.S.T.S)*
which is meant to evoke the feeling of *(Feelingful Intention)*.

1. I/We used _____
to invite the perception of _____
which is meant to evoke the feeling of _____.

2. I/We used _____
to invite the perception of _____
which is meant to evoke the feeling of _____.

3. I/We used _____
to invite the perception of _____
which is meant to evoke the feeling of _____.

4. I/We used _____
to invite the perception of _____
which is meant to evoke the feeling of _____.

5. I/We used _____
to invite the perception of _____
which is meant to evoke the feeling of _____.

Evaluation

This composition is…
❏ amazing (4) because...
❏ successful (3) because...
❏ acceptable (2) because...
❏ promising (1) because...

What would I do differently if I were to repeat this project?

Other important thoughts I have learned about music or music composition.

Figure 6.6 Critical Reflection Guide. *Source*: Created by Michele Kaschub and Janice P. Smith.

MAKING THE MOST OF LIMITED TIMEFRAMES

In the ever-present battle against the clock, class time is often given to the creation and sharing of compositions. Yet, considerable learning occurs when students analyze and discuss what they have observed in the compositions of others. In just 2–3 minutes, pairs of student can identify and draw connections between the feelingful intentions, musical expressivities, and the techniques of artistic craftsmanship used within a short piece. In just 3–5 minutes, small groups of students can describe how the choice of feelingful intentions and use of compositional techniques was designed to engage a particular audience or bring about a specific type of reaction. Brief and focused analysis and discussion help students hone their skills of perception so that they become increasingly aware of the tools and techniques available to them as they work to artistically craft music for expressive purposes. This is time well invested.

NOTES

1. Bruner, J. S. (1961). "The act of discovery." *Harvard Educational Review* 31 (1): 21–32.
2. Piaget, J. (1936). *Origins of Intelligence in the Child.* Routledge & Kegan Paul.
3. Dewey, J. (1938). *Experience & Education.* Kappa Delta Pi.
4. Deutsch, D. (2012). "Teaching gifted learners in composition." In Kaschub, M. and Smith, J. (Eds.), *Composing Our Future: Preparing Music Educators to Teach Composition.* Oxford University Press, 136.

Section 4

TEACHER GUIDES AND STUDENT *SKETCHPAGES*

Chapter 7

Teacher Guides

This section contains fifteen teacher guides designed to help those who wish to mentor middle school students as they explore composition. Each guide includes:

1. an overview of a composition project;
2. the identification of one or more National Arts Standards for Music that will be addressed within the project
3. descriptions of how to facilitate student learning throughout the compositional process;
4. examples of questions that can be used to prompt the development of compositional capacities; and
5. one or more reproducible/downloadable *Sketchpage(s)* for students to use as they create original compositions within each project.

CURRICULAR ORGANIZATION

Table 7.1 shows how projects are organized across the five different compositional genres. Each strand features one activity tailored for beginner, intermediate, and advanced middle school composers. However, all activities can be adjusted to meet the needs of students with differing levels of compositional experience and skill. Throughout each strand, middle school composers will consider the feelingful intentions, the musical expressivities, and the tools and techniques of artistic craftsmanship that suit a particular genre and project. They also will explore their creative potential as composers and come to value their own interpretations and understandings of what makes their music artistic and important.

Table 7.1 Curricular Organization by Level and Composition Strand

	Experiencing Music Composition in Middle School General Music				
	Songwriting	*Film Scoring*	*Instrumental Music*	*Electronic Music and Digital Media*	*Music Theater*
Beginner	A Songwriter's Workshop	And Now, a Public Service Announcement	Percussing Art	Light up Your Phone with a Bespoke Ringtone	Color Me Moody!
Intermediate	Haiku Opera	One Scene, Many Interpretations	Upcycled Music	Song Production	Spoken Word and Music
Advanced	Creating a Jazz Vocal	Scoring Dynamic Documentaries	Composing Idiomatic Solos	Environmental Musics	Reimagining Great Literature

Source: Michele Kaschub and Janice P. Smith.

Songwriting

The creation of songs is often one of the most enticing composition activities for young adolescents. Songs are a natural connection point in the social structure of teens and they correspond with storytelling—another creative medium that young teens tend to embrace. The three lesson projects featured in this strand invite composers to think about the ways that songs function in different genres. Students will create songs stemming from popular and contemporary practices, songs for opera, and songs drawing on the traditions of jazz as they use their own experiences to share stories that reveal both the common and unique aspects of being human.

Composition and Visual Media

Music often plays a supportive, yet critical, role in how we experience narratives. In the composition and visual media strand of the *Experiencing Music Composition* curriculum, students create public service announcements, explore how a single movie scene can be experientially altered with different musical interpretation, and how documentaries become more powerful in message when the right music is added. In each setting, composers are challenged to enhance verbal narratives with musical ones in ways that directly impact how audiences will experience the message.

Instrumental Music

Middle school musicians often have very specific musical interests. In this strand, composers are challenged to invent percussion works using visual art as a point of inspiration, compose for a solo instrument using both idiomatic and non-idiomatic musical gestures, and create original instruments and music through the processes of recycling and upcycling. These activities allow composers to connect with other arts and work with performers as they bring original compositions into being.

Electronic Music and Digital Media

Electronic music and digital media feature prominently in the lives of most adolescents. The activities of this strand capitalize on these interests by engaging composers in the creation of signature ringtones, pop song production, and exploring the complex challenges of creating music for and within specific environmental spaces. Each project develops a range of musical skills and is immediately applicable in the technological life of the compositional community.

Music Theater

Music theater is a genre that captures the imagination of middle school composers. Be it the quirky characters, classic themes, or reframing familiar tales to offer different perspectives, music theater offers something for everyone. The activities in this strand focus on creating particular moods for characters, bringing music's power to the dramatization of text, and the creation of an original production using a beloved story as a point of departure.

PROJECTS FOR BEGINNING COMPOSERS

Chapter 8

A Songwriter's Workshop

Beginner Level

Composition Strand: Songwriting

About this Project

In this lesson, students will learn an easy set of steps for creating an original song. Using their own interests as a point of inspiration, songwriters will consider the intended message of their lyrics, consider how chord patterns can invite an emotional connection point for an audience, and craft a melody and lyric that allows them to share their thoughts with the world. Students may work individually, in pairs, or in small groups. This lesson works equally well in face-to-face and online environments.

National Arts Standards for Music

Through this lesson, students will have the opportunity to:

- MU:Cr1.1.6a. Generate simple rhythmic, melodic, and harmonic phrases within AB and ABA forms that convey expressive intent.
- MU:Cr2.1.6a. Select, organize, construct, and document personal musical ideas for arrangements and compositions within AB or ABA form that demonstrate an effective beginning, middle, and ending, and convey expressive intent.
- MU:Cr2.1.6b. Use standard and/or iconic notation and/or audio/ video recording to document personal simple rhythmic phrases, melodic phrases, and two-chord harmonic musical ideas.
- MU:Cr3.1.8a. Evaluate their own work by selecting and applying criteria including appropriate application of compositional techniques, style, form, and use of sound sources.
- MU:Cr3.1.8b. Describe the rationale for refining works by explaining the choices, based on evaluation criteria.
- MU:Cr3.2.8a. Present the final version of their documented personal composition, song, or arrangement, using craftsmanship and originality to demonstrate the application of compositional techniques for creating unity and variety, tension and release, and balance to convey expressive intent.
- MU:Re7.1.6a. Select or choose music to listen to and explain the connections to specific interests or experiences for a specific purpose.
- MU:Re7.2.6a. Describe how the elements of music and expressive qualities relate to the structure of the pieces.
- MU:Re7.2.6b. Identify the context of music from a variety of genres, cultures, and historical periods.
- MU:Re8.1.6a. Describe a personal interpretation of how creators' and performers' application of the elements of music and expressive qualities, within genres and cultural and historical context, convey expressive intent.
- MU:Re9.1.8a. Apply appropriate personally developed criteria to evaluate musical works or performances.
- MU:Cn10.0.6a. Demonstrate how interests, knowledge, and skills relate to personal choices and intent when creating, performing, and responding to music.

Materials

- A *Songwriter's Listening Guide* for each student.
- A packet of *Songwriter's Sketchpages* for each composer or team of composers.
- Guitars or apps suited for producing chordal accompaniment that can produce a strumming sound or close approximation.
- A *Critical Reflection Guide* for each composer (see appendix B).

Project Time

- This project will take four to five class periods and makes a great weeklong unit.
- Students may need additional time to make a good quality recording of their work. If students have access to guitars, ukuleles, or smart devices/apps that will play chords, this project may be introduced in class, worked on at home, and then final projects shared in class.

DISCUSSION QUESTIONS TO DEVELOP COMPOSITIONAL CAPACITIES

? Feelingful Intention—What is the intended mood or character of your song? Do different sections or parts of your song invite different feelings?
? Musical Expressivity—Songs typically feature chordal patterns that repeat. This repetition can create unity, but it can also become monotonous. Which of the other MUSTS will you use to keep the listener engaged?
? Artistic Craftsmanship—Why did you select the chordal pattern or patterns that are featured in your piece? How does your strumming rhythm contribute to the style of your song? How does the shape of your melody influence the mood or mood changes within your song?

SEQUENCE OF ACTIVITIES

Phase 1—Teacher Preparation

- It is important to acknowledge the wide array of song styles and genres that may appeal to students as these will influence their work as songwriters. Ask each student to identify their favorite two to three songs, preferably by singer-songwriter types. These will provide the most useful models for this introduction to songwriting. (MU:Re7.1.6a)
- Collect student answers and do a quick sort. Are there common songs or artists? Listen to these works noting appropriateness for classroom use and potential for highlighting songwriting techniques. Pick a few songs, from different genres if possible, to use as models in class. Try to find songs that will offer a variety of techniques and insights. Songs might feature:
  ◦ Introduction
  ◦ Verse
  ◦ Pre-Chorus
  ◦ Chorus/Refrain
  ◦ Transition/Middle 8/Bridge
  ◦ Outro
  ◦ Lyrics
  ◦ Rhyme schemes
  ◦ Melodic hooks
  ◦ Rhythmic hooks
  ◦ Chordal patterns
  ◦ Major or minor tonalities
  ◦ Etc.

Phase 2—Composer Preparation: Analyzing Song Models

- Introduce the songwriting project to the class. Ask students to suggest ways to figure out how to write a song. Students will likely have a handful of ideas including listening to good songs to discover what other songwriters have done. Develop this idea by using the students' own song choices as examples.
- Distribute the *Songwriter's Listening Guide*. Invite the students to write down anything they notice about how a song is put together as the full class listens to one of the model songs that you have selected. (MU:Re7.2.6a)
- Invite students to share their observations. What is the importance of what they heard? What is the role of this component within the overall song? If necessary, listen to the song again to highlight the observation and to make sure that every student can hear and understands what is being discussed. Repeat this process with two to three songs. Take time to compare songs, styles, and techniques. (MU:Re7.2.6b)

Phase 3—Composing Songs

- Distribute all the *Sketchpages* in a songwriting packet and encourage students to begin work. It may help students to work through the first few steps together before continuing to work on their own or in their groups. (MU:Cr1.1.6a, MU:Cr2.1.6a, MU:Cr2.1.6b)
- Identify spots where you would like to check in with students. These spots should be chosen in a manner that allows students a degree of autonomy balanced with what you believe they will find to be adequate support from you. This may be at every step or every three or four steps. Discuss this with students and agree on a check-in procedure so that everyone is comfortable with the plan.
- As students work, circulate around the room, and be available to answer questions. Be aware that some students sit quietly and think through steps before outwardly making music or writing lyrics. Let them be quiet until you see no action for several minutes, then check in. The goal is to avoid disrupting good thinking! Other students will jump right into writing, strumming, and exploring their ideas. All approaches are good practice.
- At some point in each class period, take 10 minutes to run a Composers' Circle (See pages 40–41). This will allow students to solicit feedback and ideas should they become temporarily stuck in the creative process. (MU:Re7.2.6a, MU:Re8.1.6a)
- Make sure that students have a clear understanding of when their songs need to be finished. Some songwriters will work quickly; others may need more time in experimentation or refinement to achieve the results they seek. In either case, students will need to determine when their songs are finished. (MU:Cr3.1.8a, MU:Cr3.1.8b)
- When students are ready to share, reset the room to have a coffee-house vibe. Designate an area as the stage and invite students to take turns sharing their songs. If this plan seems too daunting to students, create a space where they can record their performances and then assemble the class to listen to and discuss the recordings. (MU:Cr3.2.8a)

Phase 4—Reflection and Self-Assessment

- Following the performance, students should engage in thinking critically about their learning, their compositional processes, and their musical products.
- The *Critical Reflection Guide* located in the appendix can serve as a useful tool for fostering this important skill. (MU:Re9.1.8a; MU:Cr3.1.8a; MU:Cr3.1.8b; MU:Cn10.0.6a)

Optional Extension

Another way to approach this lesson is to select a particular stylistic genre to explore. Students might survey pop songs, country western songs, reggae, and others. An exploration of several different genres could provide a foundation for a course focusing on songwriting.

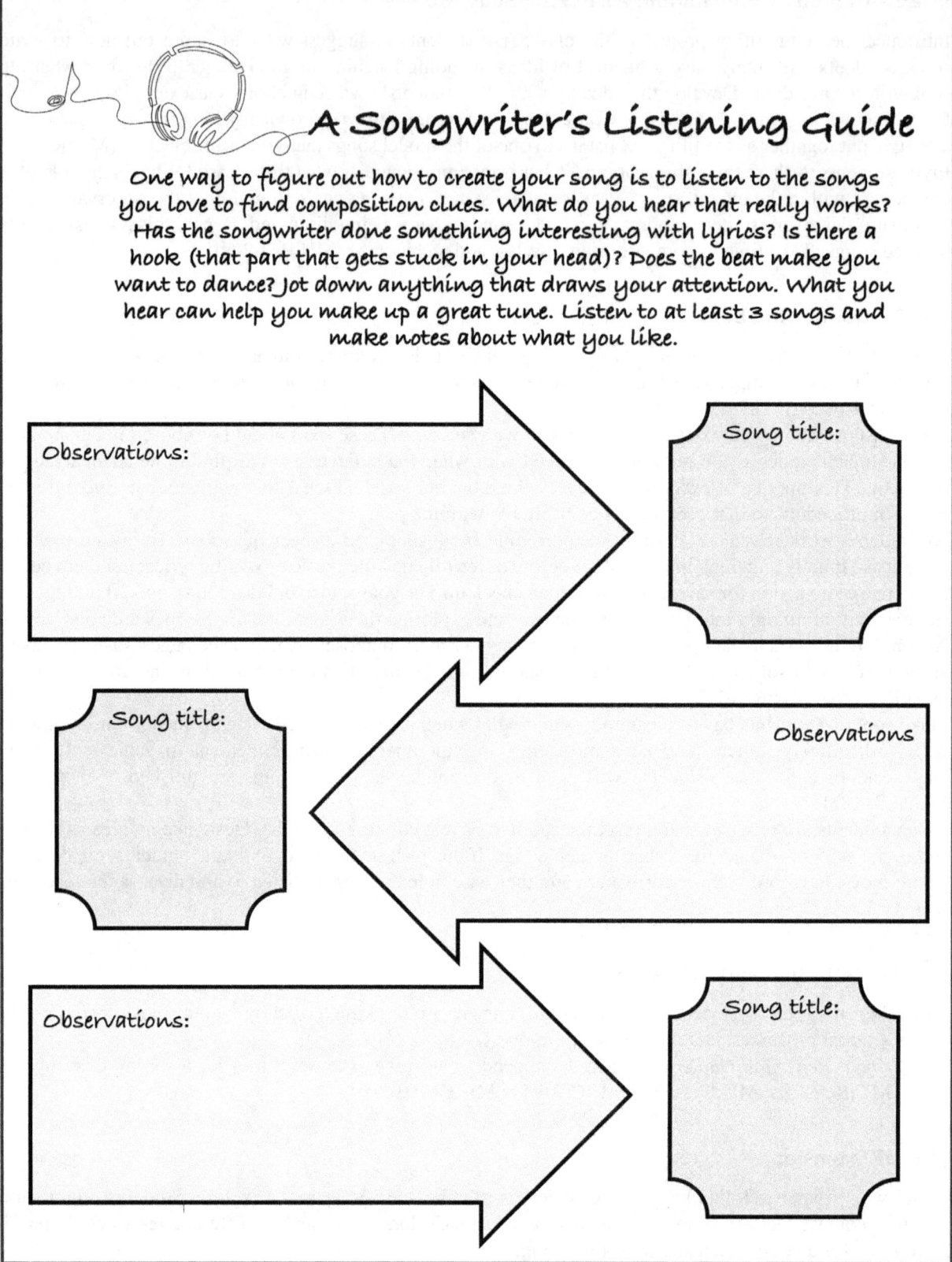

Source: Created by Michele Kaschub and Janice P. Smith with images from iStock/Credit: Tetiana Lazunova.

A Songwriter's Workshop

Have you ever heard a great song and wondered how anyone could create a song like that? The process is not a secret. Songwriting requires just a few things: a good idea, some exploration, a little practice, and a bit of persistence. In this project, you will learn a few steps to follow to create a song. These steps are suggestions to help organize your work. After you've written a few songs you may develop a different writing style. That's OK! For now, try this songwriting plan.

① Pick a topic, image, or word that is at the very heart of your song. Write it in the center of the song web.

② As you think about this idea, add a few words in the linked ovals. What is the mood of the song? Which M.U.S.T.S. shape the expressivity of the song? Are there any particular sounds that would be good to use in the song?

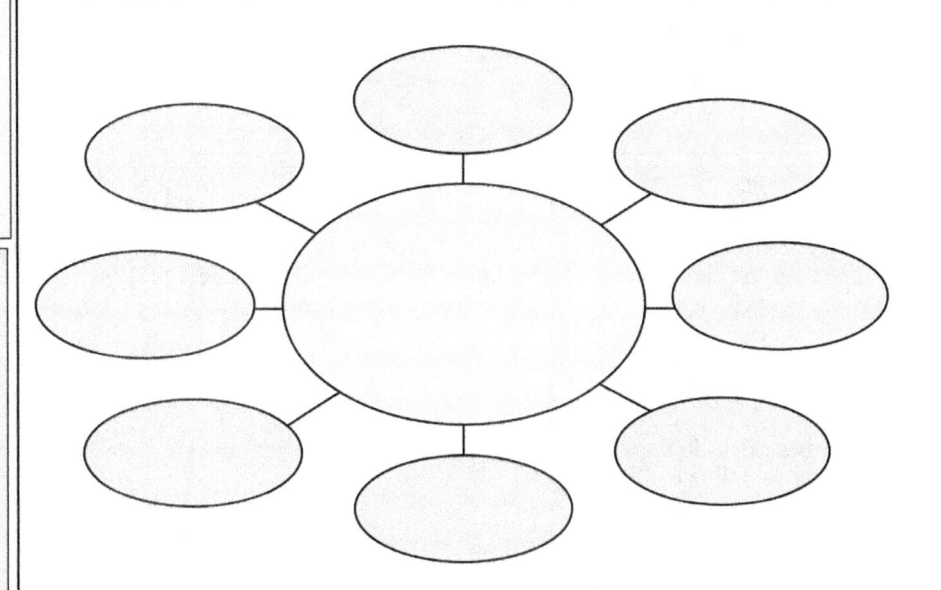

③ Write a sentence that answers, "What is the message of this song?"

④ Convert your message to a title. Using an image *(home)* and/or an action *(run)* can anchor or energize your song *(Running for Home)*.

My song title: _____

⑤ Jot your lyric ideas in the white space around the song web. What do you want to say to your listeners? What might your audience want to know? What do you feel about your topic? Why do you feel that way? If you are telling a story, what has happened and what might happen next? Try to think of one question that gets to the very heart of your song and one more question for each verse that you create. As you write lyrics, consider the questions are you trying to answer in each section.

Chorus question: _____

Verse 1 question: _____

Verse 2 question: _____

Source: Created by Michele Kaschub and Janice P. Smith with images from iStock/Credit: Koh Sze Kiat.

A Songwriter's Workshop – page 2

Let's think about music. Your song might use a single chord that conveys the mood you hope capture or a home (tonic) and away (dominant) chord. Guitars are useful for this or you might try an online guitar app like https://www.apronus.com/music/onlineguitar.htm which will allow you to play your progression live or record it and play it back. Common patterns might include alternating between D (home/tonic) and A (away/dominant); D-Em-G-A-D; Dm-Em-G-A-D; and D-G-A-Bm. Experiment until you find a progression that fits the mood of your song.

Note a few progressions that you like:

Writing lyrics that convey your message over the chords you like is the next challenge. Songwriters often find it helpful to begin with the chorus as it can provide unity to a song.

Use your best ideas in the chorus. Say each line out loud. Say them again with the emotion you want to convey. Notice how you say each line. Does it seem to have a natural rhythm? If you like this rhythm, keep it. If you think a word needs to be longer or shorter to have the right emotional impact, make adjustments.

Speak the line over your chord progression. Begin to notice where your voice naturally rises and falls. Stretch these natural tendencies into a melody. Once the melody solidifies, record yourself singing the melody over the chord progression. Recording provides a safety net for your memory so you won't lose track of your ideas as you move on to work on your verses.

A lead sheet is the text of your song with chord names written above the word/syllable where they are played. Jot the lead sheet for your chorus here:

Source: Created by Michele Kaschub and Janice P. Smith.

A Songwriter's Workshop – page 3

⑨ Start work on your first verse. Use the same approach here as you used with chorus, working line by line until Verse 1 is finished. Record it. Repeat this process for Verse 2.

⑩ Draw the lead sheet for Verse 1 here:

⑪ Draw the lead sheet for Verse 2 here:

⑫ One common song form is: introduction/verse/chorus/verse/chorus/bridge/chorus/outro. This form adds three parts to what you have already made.

The **introduction** sets the tone for your song. It can be simple or dramatic. Some songwriters play a single chord, others play through a progression used at some point in the song.

What feeling or mood do you want to establish?

Try a few different starters. Describe your intro or write your chords here:

Source: Created by Michele Kaschub and Janice P. Smith.

A Songwriter's Workshop – page 4

The **bridge** sits between two choruses and adds an extra dose of emotion to your song. It might provide the audience with additional information. The melody of the bridge should be different from that of the verses or chorus and the chord progression may change to kick up the emotional quality of your song. What do you plan to do?

The **outro** closes the song. Songwriters often repeat just the last line of the chorus. This can be done with or without the lyrics. Sometimes a "repeat and fade" approach is used or the final chord is simply repeated one more time. Experiment to find out what makes the most sense for the ending of your song. Describe how your song will end.

FINISHING UP

- ❑ Play your song for a few friends. What do they like? What suggestions do they make?
- ❑ Are you comfortable with every lyric, note, and line of your song? If so, you are done! If not, revise and rework the music until your song feels right to you.
- ❑ Use a computer, phone, or tablet to record your song. Sing it like you are telling the story to someone. It may take a few tries to get the recording just right. Take a break if you start to get a little frustrated. Creating a really good performance is hard work!
- ❑ Lock it in! Make a final recording of your work.

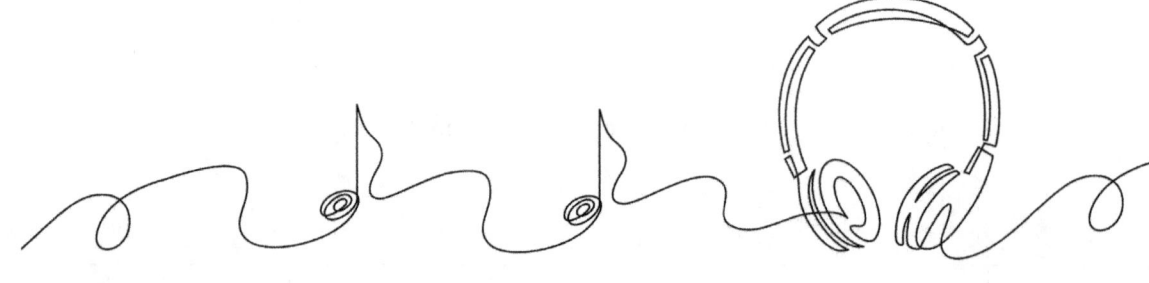

Source: Created by Michele Kaschub and Janice P. Smith with images from iStock/Credit: Tetiana Lazunova.

Chapter 9

And Now, A Public Service Announcement

Beginner Level

Composition Strand: Film Scoring

About this Project

Middle school students are exposed to an endless stream of information from television, videos, online hosting sites, and other forms of social media. Developing the skills necessary to analyze and critically think about these messages allows students to better understand and respond to the information they receive. Music is often a component of these videos, yet many students have given little thought to why the music was chosen or the impact that it has on how people internalize the message. Producing a public service announcement (PSA) is a way to involve students with topics and issues that are important to them. This activity will help students think about how information can be presented and how they might use music to further their own persuasive arguments.

Note: This teacher guide is designed to facilitate the creation of an original, student-created PSA. However, if a shorter project timeframe is desired, students can compose music to fit an existing PSA, such as those housed at archive.org. Teachers can use editing software to remove the soundtrack but may wish to preserve the script for student to perform as one of their recorded tracks. Students might also create a new script for an existing PSA. Teachers following this plan will use most of Phase 1 to introduce the project and then jump to Phase 5 where students compose the underscore for their PSA.

National Arts Standards for Music

This lesson presents students with an opportunity to:

- MU:Cr2.1.6a. Select, organize, construct, and document personal musical ideas for arrangements and compositions within AB or ABA form that demonstrate an effective beginning, middle, and ending, and convey expressive intent.
- MU:Cr2.1.7a. Select, organize, develop, and document personal musical ideas for arrangements, songs, and compositions within AB, ABA, or theme and variation forms that demonstrate unity and variety and convey expressive intent.
- MU:Cr3.1.8a. Evaluate their own work by selecting and applying criteria including appropriate application of compositional techniques, style, form, and use of sound sources.
- MU:Cr3.1.8b. Describe the rationale for refining works by explaining the choices, based on evaluation criteria.
- MU:Cr3.2.8a. Present the final version of their documented personal composition, song, or arrangement, using craftsmanship and originality to demonstrate the application of compositional techniques for creating unity and variety, tension and release, and balance to convey expressive intent.
- MU:Re7.2.6a. Describe how the elements of music and expressive qualities relate to the structure of the pieces.

- MU:Re9.1.8a. Apply appropriate personally developed criteria to evaluate musical works or performances.
- MU:Cn10.0.6a. Demonstrate how interests, knowledge, and skills relate to personal choices and intent when creating, performing, and responding to music.
- MU:Cn11.0.6a. Demonstrate understanding of relationships between music and the other arts, other disciplines, varied contexts, and daily life.

Materials

- A packet of PSA *Sketchpages*
- Software or apps for creating and editing music (Audacity, GarageBand, Musescore), slideshows (Keynote, Powerpoint, Prezi), or videos (iMovie, MovieMaker)
- A *Critical Reflections Guide* for each composer (see appendix B)

Project Time

- The full project will take four to five classes to complete.
- If students are using an existing PSA, the project can be completed in one to two class periods.

DISCUSSION QUESTIONS TO DEVELOP COMPOSITIONAL CAPACITIES

? Feelingful Intention—What feeling is the composer trying to invite the viewer to experience? How does the music paint the emotional journey of experiencing the problem that is the focus of the PSA?
? Musical Expressivity—How can the MUSTS be activated to increase the feelingful impact of a PSA?
? Artistic Craftsmanship—What compositional techniques will be used to support that experience?

SEQUENCE OF ACTIVITIES

Phase 1—Create Common Ground

- To initiate this project, play a video of a PSA and ask students to explain what a PSA is and the purpose of PSAs. Note: An extensive collection of professionally made PSAs can be found at https://www.psacentral.org/campaigns.
- Watch a few more PSAs together. Invite students to create a list of things they find to be effective in different PSAs. Is it the message (dialogue or text), the actors, the imagery, the music? Why are these components of the PSA impactful? If watching a PSA with music, would it be equally impactful without music? Conversely, if watching a PSA without music, would it have greater impact if music were added? Invite students to describe the music they might add and why they think that style or character of music would advance the message of the PSA. (MU:Re7.2.6a)
- Introduce the project. Explain that the class will be making a collection of PSAs. Students will be divided into teams of five to six students to produce either PSA of 30 seconds (appropriate for Facebook) or a series of shorter videos totaling 30 seconds in length (perhaps appropriate for Instagram or Snapchat). Both formats would also be appropriate for the school's closed-circuit broadcast system.
- Each PSA must have a clear message, written script, and music. Student will need to act as researchers, writers, videographers, and composers as this project unfolds.

Phase 2—Identify a Topic and Conduct Research

- Move students into production teams and have them make a list of issues that they are concerned about. These may be personal, social, education (school-focused, school-situated), or community issues. Once the students

have drafted a list, have them discuss the merits of each issue as the potential focal point of a PSA. This activity is crucial in that it establishes both the team and product focus and will serve as a motivating force if the team is passionate about their topic. (MU:Cn11.0.6a/7a/8a)
- Distribute *Sketchpage 1: PSA Concept Development* and encourage teams to identify their project focus (MU:Cr2.1.6a) by considering these questions:
    a. What is the key message that PSA will deliver?
    b. Who is the main message of the PSA intended to reach?
    c. What facts will be shared in the PSA?
    d. What action do you hope viewers will take after watching the PSA?
    e. Are there current new stories or events that make the PSA particularly relevant? How might this connection help attract eyes and encourage others to discuss and share the PSA?
    f. What will our hashtag be? #betterwithahashtag
- Each team should research their topic to develop a strong base of factual information and a personal understanding of the topic. This will be critical in the development of a tightly messaged script.
- Guide students in translating facts about their topic into a list of major points to be conveyed in the PSA.
- Remind students that the goal is to create an impactful message. People tend to remember just one or two points from a 30-second message. If multiple short video formats are used, one point per video may be impactful, but repeating points to "hammer the message home" is another approach that may be effective. Students should also consider using acronyms, rhymes, and other devices to help boost key point retention.

Phase 3—Creating PSA Storyboard

- Distribute *Sketchpage 2: Storyboarding* to guide students in developing their script, list of images, and sound concept. Students will need multiple copies of this *Sketchpage.*
- Teams should first identify how they will package and distribute their PSA. For example, if the message is intended for peers, what is the most popular social media app that can deliver video and how long can that video be? Is a 30-second video the right length for their message/audience or would a series of shorter videos, maybe just a few seconds in length and released over several days via Instagram, Snapchat, or comparable platform be better for accessing their intended audience?
- Invite students to decide how they will approach text delivery. Will there be a narrator, a first-person perspective, dialogue, or text projection without a speaker?
- Once these decisions are made, students should craft their script. Encourage students to:
    a. use simple, conversational language and to avoid unnecessary jargon.
    b. keep sentences concise and on-point.
    c. read the completed script out loud, speaking slowly and clearly while they check its length.
- Students should begin to fill in the three columns of the *Sketchpage*. This may be done as they write the script or in stages as naturally suits their working processes.

Phase 4—Making the Video

- Teammates need to discuss how the video for their PSA will be made. Some teams may choose to record videos of themselves acting out scenes, some may decide to use collections of still or moving images with narrations, and others may decide to work within presentation software to create movies without the use video or spoken audio. All forms are acceptable as long as students can justify their artistic choices.
- Students can use the *Sketchpage 2* to add notes for each scene. Remind students that scenes may be dialogue or the delivery of a series of images.
- If students are filming video or taking photographs, they may need to collect props or shoot on location. Remind students that some locations may have rules about photography and that they should seek permission (you may need to help them) before taking photographs or shooting video.
- If students are using pre-existing images or pre-recorded videos in their PSAs, they should honor copyright laws.

- Build time: Students assembling PSAs in presentation software will need time to create their slideshows. They may also need time to record spoken audio tracks. Students shooting video will need time to edit and align clips using appropriate software or apps.

Phase 5—Creating the Underscore

- Each team should view their video and decide how music might be used to invite the audience to make a stronger connection with the message of the PSA. The underscore is not there to tell the story already present in the text and visuals but serves to create a feelingful impression which impacts how the audience reacts to the message. Note: If students are completing the shorter form of this project, distribute *Sketchpage 2* and have teams add the script and describe the visual images of their PSA before beginning work on the underscore.
- Encourage students to identify the feelingful intentions, musical expressivities, and tools of artistic craftsmanship that they will utilize in each scene. This can be done before or while they are composing the music. Students who are creating a series of short videos may want to think carefully about unity: What will connect their videos? Does their PSA need a title theme or some other musical device to help connect its segments? (MU:Cr2.1.7a)
- When students have composed their musical material, they will need to align video and underscore in movie editing software.

Phase 6—Composers' Circle

- Students need an opportunity to market test their PSAs. For videos intended for peers, a ready-made audience exists in the class. If videos are aimed at adults, other teachers, parents, and community members might be invited into class to offer feedback. If visitors are being invited into the classroom, take a moment to explain how Composers' Circles work, share guidelines, and set clear expectations for how feedback is offered.
- Provide students with some time to think about the feedback they have received and what they observed in the PSAs developed by other teams. A brief period of time should be set aside for minor revisions and final edits. (MU:Re9.1.8a)

Phase 7—Go live!

- Completed PSAs can now be shared as planned. Videos may be uploaded to a class website, shared through social media, or unveiled at a school or community event. If the PSA has logical partners in the community, have students meet with representatives and ask them to share the PSA on their website and through their social media outlets. (MU:Cr3.2.8a)

Phase 8—Reflections and Self-Assessment

- Live discussion: After the PSAs have been shared and in circulation for a few days, invite students to share their experiences. How did people react to their PSA? Do they believe that the PSA reached its target audience? Has any conversation started around the PSA? (MU:Cr3.1.8a) Have they witnessed any of the outcomes they were hoping for as the PSA was planned? (MU:Cr3.1.8b)
- The *Critical Reflections Guide* located in the appendix can serve as a useful tool for fostering this important skill. (MU:Re9.1.8a; MU:Cr3.1.8a; MU:Cr3.1.8b; MU:Cn10.0.6a)

Optional Extension

This same project can be completed with a focus on political advertisements. Have students study the music of both positive and negative ads. Then, have them take the same video footage and compose an underscore that is positive and a second that is negative. Students may add new narration to further skew the advertisement to one perspective or another.

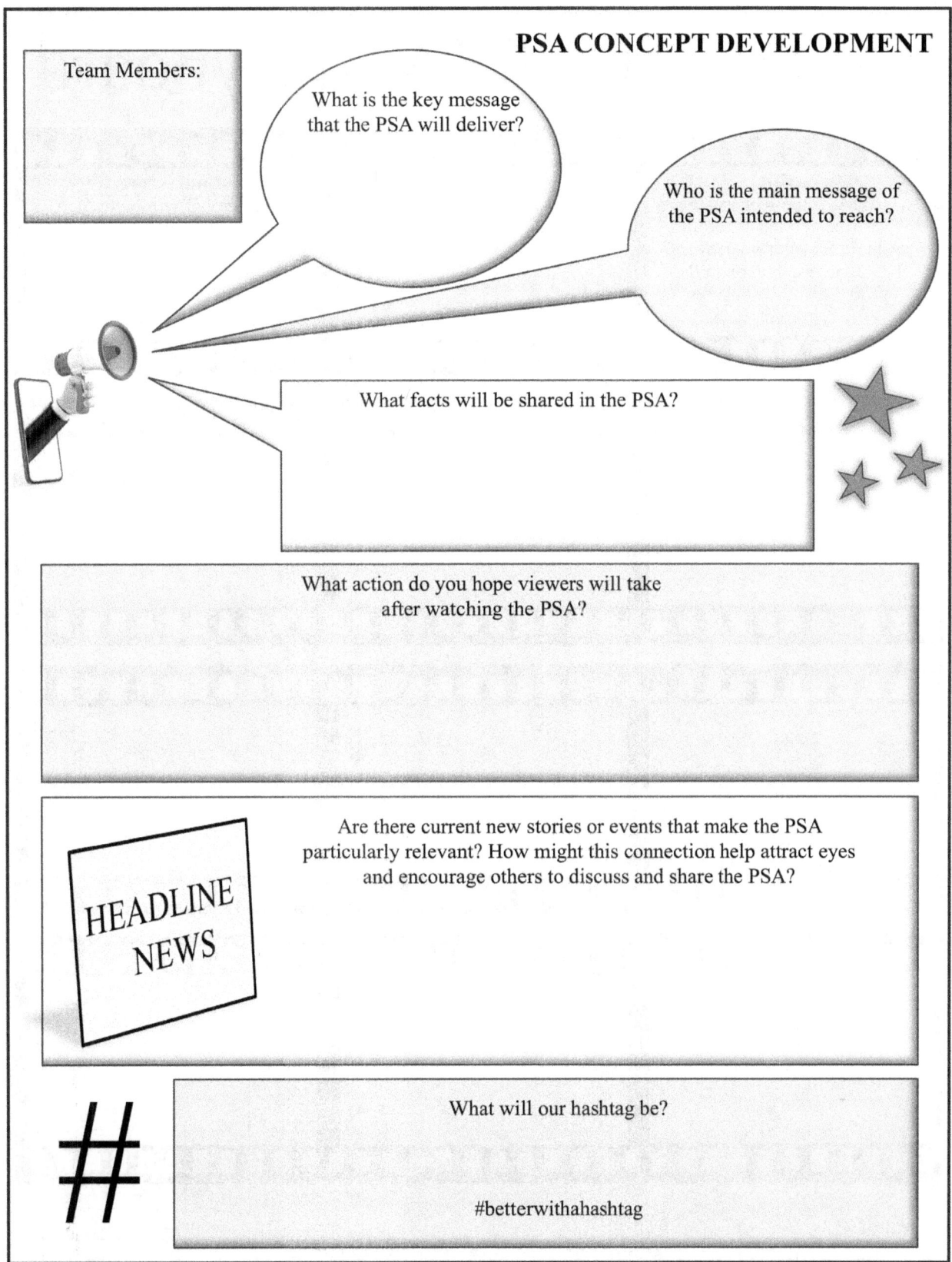

Source: Created by Michele Kaschub and Janice P. Smith with images from iStock/Credit: Rinat Khairitdinov.

Chapter 9

Create Your PSA Storyboard

Script
What is the scenario? Describe actions of actors; write dialogue or voiceovers. Dialogue might explain the problem and voiceovers often present facts.

Visual Imagery
What will show on the screen? Describe how images will show the problem or facts.

Underscore
What feeling will be invited? How will that feeling be experienced (MUSTS)? What compositional techniques will be used to support that experience?

Creator/s: _____

Source: Created by Michele Kaschub and Janice P. Smith.

Chapter 10

Percussing Art

Beginner Level

Composition Strand: Instrumental Music

About this Project

Beginning in the early twentieth century with the paintings of Wassily Kandinsky, many artists turned to the world of music to find inspiration for their own works (i.e., Stravkinsky's *Rite of Spring* inspired Kandinsky's *Composition VIII*). Painters exploring this approach to making art believed that senses could be blended so that one mode of sensory perception could manifest itself as sensory output in another mode. Kandinsky, Paul Klee, and others sought to explore color in relation to timbre, harmony, and elemental constructs. Later artists such as Jackson Pollock explored the relationship between color and tempo, while Morgan Russell used the color wheel to explore and identify what he came to term as "color chords" in painting. Eventually these trends extended to the world of jazz, where the piano music of Earl Hines and Fats Waller influenced the paintings of Stuart Davis. Most recently, artists with synesthesia (a condition where sound is experienced visually as colors) have begun to paint what they experience visually as they listen to music. Melissa McCracken's interpretations of Radiohead's "Lucky" and John Mayer's "Gravity" can be seen at https://mymodernmet.com/melissa-mccracken-synethesia-paintings/

In this project, students will flip the art-from-music model to use visual art as a point of inspiration for the creation of musical works. Visual art can be a powerful prompt for novice composers as the internal structures of an artwork can be used in a literal way to serve as music score or may suggest overarching feelings or moods that shape how a composition is constructed. Working in small groups, students will consider the rhythm and affect of a painting for which they will create a partner-composition. Both pieces are to evoke a similar feelingful response with viewers and listeners.

National Arts Standards for Music

This lesson presents students with an opportunity to:

- MU:Cr2.1.6a. Select, organize, construct, and document personal musical ideas for arrangements and compositions within AB or ABA form that demonstrate an effective beginning, middle, and ending, and convey expressive intent.
- MU:Cr3.1.8a. Evaluate their own work by selecting and applying criteria including appropriate application of compositional techniques, style, form, and use of sound sources.
- MU:Cr3.1.8b. Describe the rationale for refining works by explaining the choices, based on evaluation criteria.
- MU:Cr3.2.8a. Present the final version of their documented personal composition, song, or arrangement, using craftsmanship and originality to demonstrate the application of compositional techniques for creating unity and variety, tension and release, and balance to convey expressive intent.
- MU:Re7.2.6a. Describe how the elements of music and expressive qualities relate to the structure of the pieces.

- MU:Re9.1.8a. Apply appropriate personally developed criteria to evaluate musical works or performances.
- MU:Cn10.0.6a. Demonstrate how interests, knowledge, and skills relate to personal choices and intent when creating, performing, and responding to music.
- MU:Cn11.0.6a. Demonstrate understanding of relationships between music and the other arts, other disciplines, varied contexts, and daily life.

Materials

- A *Percussing Art Sketchpage*.
- Image of one abstract painting for each small group; an Internet search for "abstract paintings" will yield many examples that are geometric and non-representational.
- Variety of percussion instruments; body percussion may also be used.
- A copy of the *Critical Reflections Guide* for each composer (see appendix B).

Project Time

- It will take approximately 50 minutes to compose, share, and reflect on this project.

DISCUSSION QUESTIONS TO DEVELOP COMPOSITIONAL CAPACITIES

? Feelingful Intention—What descriptive words best capture the essence of your composition? What feeling would an audience be left with after hearing this piece?
? Musical Expressivity—Which of the MUSTS were most important in interpreting the artwork that served as an inspiration for this composition? Describe how the identified MUSTS impact the piece.
? Artistic Craftsmanship—How do the sounds of the composition represent specific elements of the artwork or suggest do they suggest a broader character, feeling, or mood?

SEQUENCE OF ACTIVITIES

Phase 1—Considering Sight and Sound

- Open this lesson by asking students if they ever draw or doodle while listening to music. What do they draw? Why do they think that listening to music invites doodling? Do they see connections between what they are listening to and what they draw? Can they describe or explain these connections. (MU:Cn10.0.6a)
- Without revealing the song title or composer/performer, project Melissa McCracken's interpretations of John Mayer's *Gravity* (https://mymodernmet.com/melissa-mccracken-synethesia-paintings/) where students can view it. Ask them to describe the artwork. What mood does it invite? Why? Can they think of a piece of music that the artwork might fit? Why do they make this connection? (MU:Cn11.0.6a)
- Have students listen to *Gravity* as they look at McCracken's painting. Do they perceive any connections between the song and painting? (MU:CN11.0.6a) Questions that may prompt this critical analysis include:
  ○ Is there a connection between the feelingful intentions of the two works?
  ○ Which of the MUSTS are most present?
  ○ Are there elemental constructs (use of color, shapes, brushstrokes) that correspond with musical sounds? Explain that McCracken has a unique condition that allows her to see colors as she listens to music, but that there is a long history of artists, without that condition, painting to music.

Phase 2—Composition Time

- Introduce today's project as a "flip-the-script" activity in which students will create an original composition based on a painting.
- Divide the class into small groups of four or five members each. Distribute one abstract painting to each group and one *Percussing Art Sketchpage* to each composer. Once students have examined their artwork, allow them to gather a collection of percussion instruments. (MU:Cr2.1.6a; MU:Re7.2.6a)
- Students will need 15–20 minutes to compose their piece. To manage decibel levels, advise students to work at a *pianissimo* dynamic.
- Note: Notation is not necessary unless students make notes spontaneously or request staff or other paper. Encourage students to do whatever they need to do to recall their pieces.

Phase 3—Performance and Critical Listening

- Each team should have an opportunity to perform their work for the class.
- Audience members should be ready to identify a musical impression made by the piece and which of the MUSTS helped to evoke that impression. Listeners should also be able to identify compositional techniques used by the composers. (MU:Cr3.2.8a)
- Following each performance, the following questions might be asked to facilitate reflection:
  - Audience: What descriptive words best capture your experience of this piece?
  - Composer: Which of the MUSTS were most important in the creation of your piece?
  - Composer: How was [specific MUSTS pair] shaped to match the artwork that served as your inspiration? What sounds did you make to achieve that idea?
  - Audience: For you, how did the sounds of the composition connect to the artwork? [Note: Ask this question of multiple students and discuss how/why their answers are same/different.]
  - Composer: Did the sounds of the composition represent specific elements in the artwork? Please, explain.
  - Audience: How did the overall mood of the music capture the broader character, feeling, or mood offered by the painting?

Phase 4—Reflection and Self-Assessment

- The *Critical Reflections Guide* located in the appendix can serve as a useful tool for fostering this important skill. (MU:Re9.1.8a; MU:Cr3.1.8a; MU:Cr3.1.8b; MU:Cn10.0.6a)

Optional Extension

Additional paintings can be used to increase the challenge level of this project. Provide students with three to five paintings that they sequence in an order that makes sense to them. The students then create a composition that reflects the emotional journey of the storyboard that they have arranged.

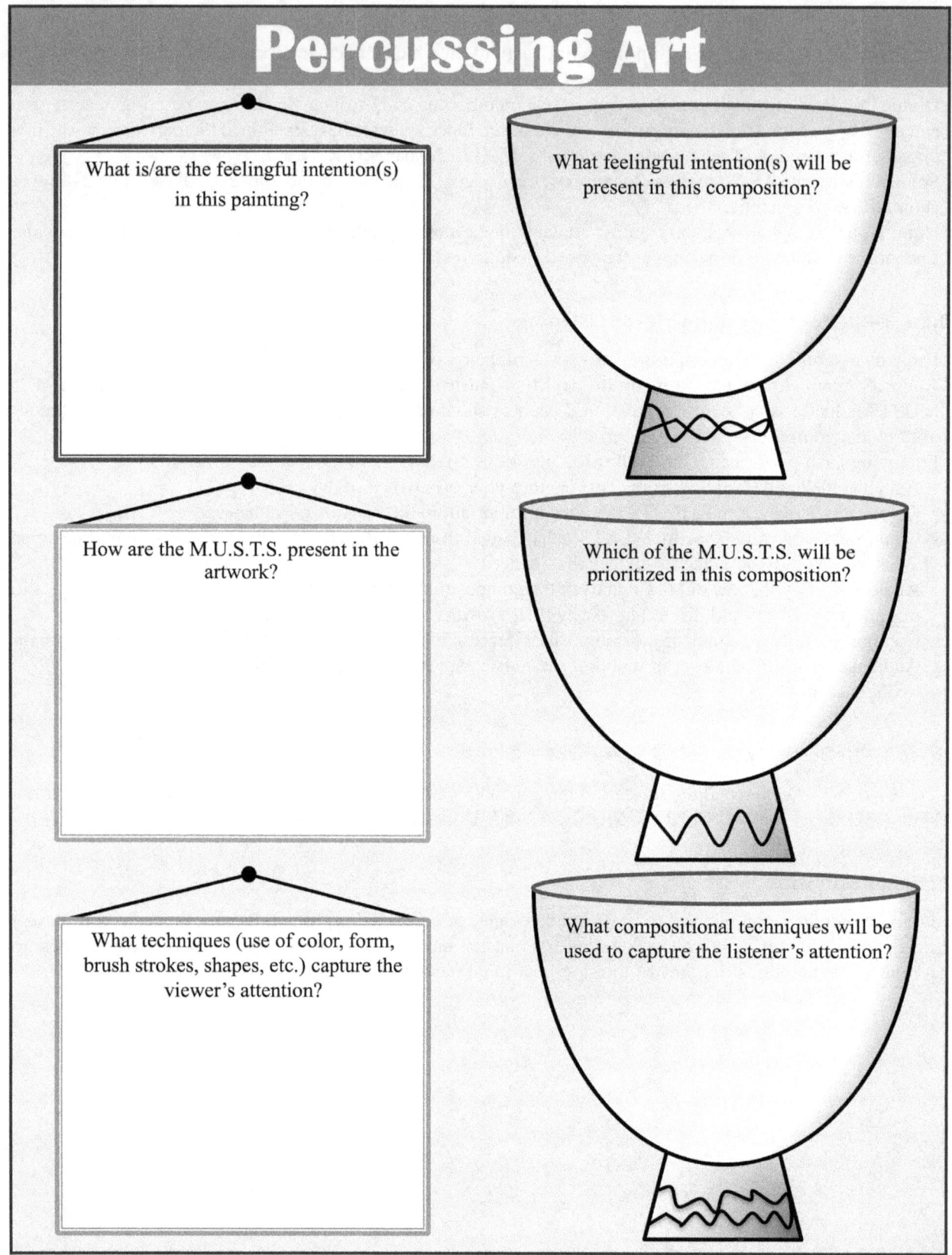

Source: Created by Michele Kaschub and Janice P. Smith.

Chapter 11

Light Up Your Phone with a Bespoke Ringtone

Beginner Level

Composition Strand: Electronic Music and Digital Media

About this Project

A unique way to present oneself to world in the socio-digital age is to use a bespoke ringtone. This compositional miniature can set one phone apart from the rest or might be gifted to family and friends as a musical calling card.

This project will invite students to consider how they might best represent themselves in a 30-second sound window. They will begin this project by identifying the characteristics of effective ringtones and how ringtones are structured. Students then will create a ringtone that reflects their unique spirit and personality. The project concludes with students learning how to convert file types and upload original ringtones to phones.

National Arts Standards for Music

This lesson presents students with an opportunity to:

- MU:Cr1.1.7a. Generate rhythmic, melodic, and harmonic phrases and variations over harmonic accompaniments within AB, ABA, or theme and variation forms that convey expressive intent.
- MU:Cr3.1.8a. Evaluate their own work by selecting and applying criteria including appropriate application of compositional techniques, style, form, and use of sound sources.
- MU:Cr3.1.8b. Describe the rationale for refining works by explaining the choices, based on evaluation criteria.
- MU:Cr3.2.8a. Present the final version of their documented personal composition, song, or arrangement, using craftsmanship and originality to demonstrate the application of compositional techniques for creating unity and variety, tension and release, and balance to convey expressive intent.
- MU:Re7.1.6a. Select or choose music to listen to and explain the connections to specific interests or experiences for a specific purpose.
- MU:Re7.2.6a. Describe how the elements of music and expressive qualities relate to the structure of the pieces.
- MU:Re9.1.8a. Apply appropriate personally developed criteria to evaluate musical works or performances.
- MU:Cn10.0.6a. Demonstrate how interests, knowledge, and skills relate to personal choices and intent when creating, performing, and responding to music.

Materials

- A *Ringtone Planner Sketchpage*
- Computer/device with notation and/or loop-based software program/apps
- Audio recording and editing software/apps

- Cell phone
- Instructions for converting MP3 files to ringtone on brand-specific phones. Note: Each phone brand may use a slightly different set of steps to move, process, and convert MP3 files. Directions for specific brands are widely available on the Internet. For efficiency, ask students what brands of phones they have and prepare instructions for each brand for students to reference as they work.
- A copy of the *Critical Reflections Guide* for each composer (see appendix B)

Project Time

- Approximately one to two class periods will be needed for this project. Some aspects may be completed as homework.

DISCUSSION QUESTIONS TO DEVELOP COMPOSITIONAL CAPACITIES

? Feelingful Intention—If you have to describe your personality, spirit, or character in a single word, what would it be? What might that sound like?
? Musical Expressivity—Which of the MUSTS will be most useful in bringing about the feelingful quality of your ringtone? Will there be a lot of motion? Will there be changes in sound quality through the use of different instruments or other sounds? What might be the role of tension?
? Artistic Craftsmanship—Ringtones are, in some ways, similar to the "hooks" in a pop song; the musical idea has to be interesting and immediately memorable. What sounds will be most effective when presented in a short time frame?

SEQUENCE OF ACTIVITIES

Phase 1—Ringtones as Mini-Compositions

- Engage students in a discussion about ringtones. Here are some prompt questions to get the discussion started:
  - What are characteristics of an effective ringtone? (MU:Re7.1.6a)
    - It gets your attention without getting the attention of everyone within a 50-yard radius of you.
    - It is insistent and makes you feel like you need to answer the phone.
    - It is easy to hear because it uses higher pitches that cut through loud, rumbling noises like those in crowded community spaces.
  - Q: How are ringtones structured? (MU:Re7.2.6a)
    - Ideas are organized to fit within a 30-second time span.
    - Some ringtones are built of non-repetitive music.
    - Some ringtones feature a longer musical idea followed by several repetitions of a shorter part of that idea.
    - Some ringtones use tiny bursts of sound repeated with increasing frequency or increasing dynamic intensity to get your attention.
    - Building tension across time is a common feature. The tension is released when the phone stops ringing.
  - Q: Does anyone use a special ringtone to identify a friend or family member? If so, why did you pick the ringtone that you have associated with that person?
  - Q: Have you ever thought about creating your own signature ringtone? Why might someone want to create an original ringtone? (MU:Cn10.0.6a)
    - If you use it as a default on your own phone, you will recognize that your phone is ringing because no one will have your ringtone.
    - A ringtone that represents you can be gifted to friends and family so that they will know when their phone rings that you are calling.

Phase 2—Introduce the Project

Distribute the *Ringtone Planner Sketchpage* and briefly introduce the project.

- Each student will create a 30-second ringtone. The *Sketchpage* provides visual models and guides students to think about how their ringtone might sound. (MU:Cr1.1.7a)
- Students can use any music-making software, app, or acoustic instruments and recording device capable of saving their creation as an MP3 file. (Reminder: Steps from here require locating directions for specific phone brands.)
- Each student will save their tiny compositions as an MP3 file.
- At this point, let students know how they will turn their MP3 file into a ringtone.
  - Option 1: If students can use their phones at school:
    - Guide students in uploading their MP3 files to their own music libraries.
    - Provide students with phone-brand-specific instructions as to how to convert their MP3 file to a ringtone file. Instructions for doing this can be found on the Internet.
  - Option 2: If students are not allowed to use their phones in class:
    - Create a shared folder where students can upload their compositions, or use another means for transferring students' composition files, saved as MP3s, to a platform which they can access outside of school.
    - Provide students with instructions for accessing their files and completing the project at home.

Phase 3—Sharing and Discussion

- Each student should have an opportunity to share his or her ringtone with the class. Encourage students to share their one-word description of themselves and then play their ringtone. (MU:Cr3.2.8a) Ask questions that prompt critical and reflective thinking after each ringtone is shared:
  - To the composer: Why do you believe the sounds you chose match the idea of [insert their descriptive word]?
  - To the composer: How did you structure your ringtone?
  - To the audience: Who can tell us what they hear in this ringtone that suggests [insert the descriptive word offered by the composer]?
  - To the audience: Who can describe the form (organizational structure) of this ringtone?
  - To either: Which of the MUSTS was most influential in this ringtone?
  - To either: How is this ringtone crafted to be catchy to the ear?

Phase 4—Reflection and Self-Assessment

- The *Critical Reflections Guide* located in the appendix can serve as a useful tool for fostering this important skill. (MU:Re9.1.8a; MU:Cr3.1.8a; MU:Cr3.1.8b; MU:Cn10.0.6a)

Optional Extension

Once students have created an original ringtone thinking about their own signature style, they might create additional ringtones for family members or friends. These miniature compositions can be sent via email to intended recipients who can then convert the file and upload it following the specifications of their own phone or other smart devices.

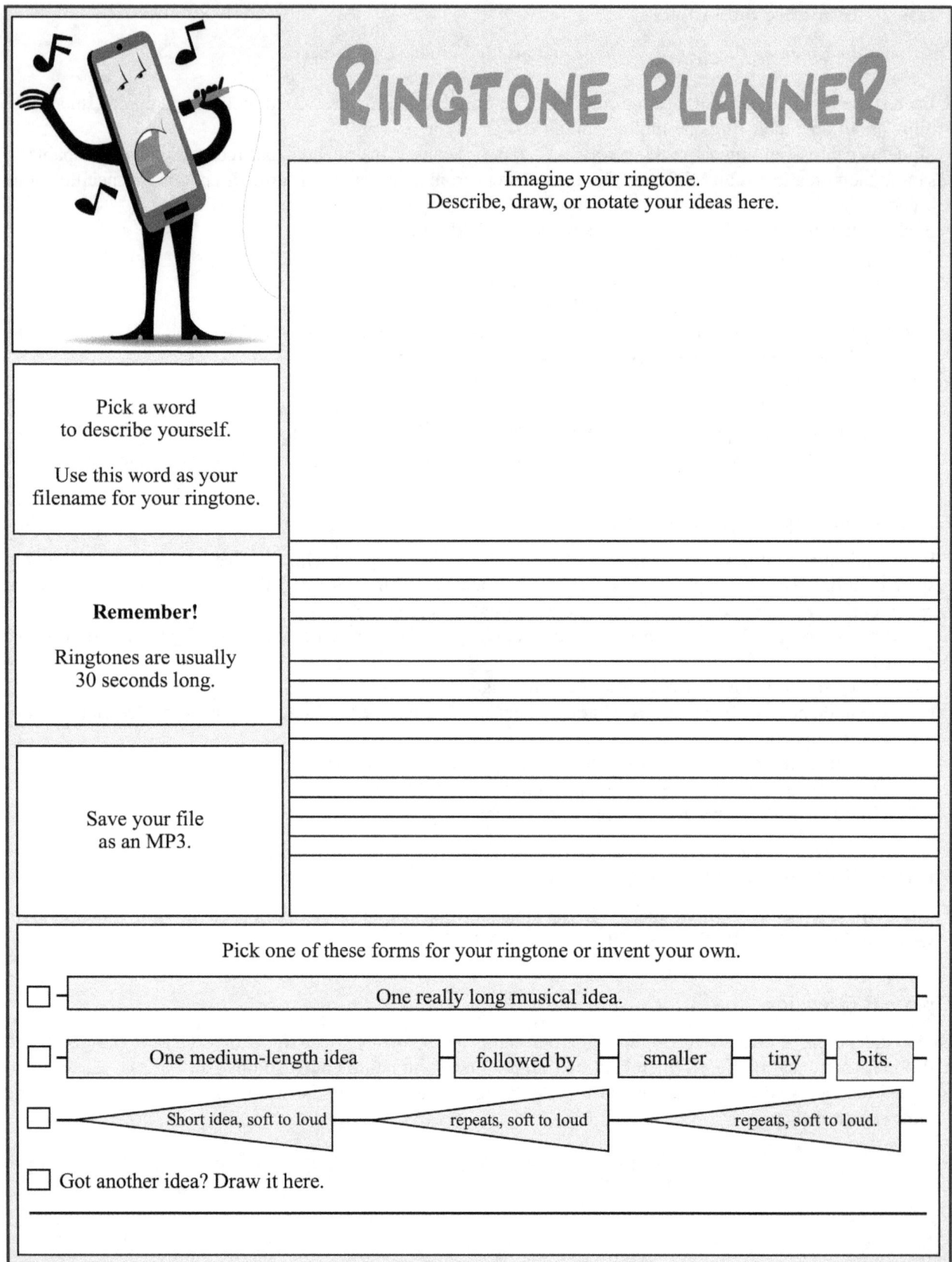

Source: Created by Michele Kaschub and Janice P. Smith with images from iStock/Credit: Planet Flem.

Chapter 12

Color Me Moody!

Beginner Level

Composition Strand: Music Theater

About this Project

This project invites students to invent a character by drawing on the feeling or mood evoked by a particular color. Students will work in small groups to write a poem personifying a color and then compose music to accompany a dramatic reading of their poem.

National Arts Standards for Music

This lesson presents students with an opportunity to:

- MU:Cr1.1.8a. Generate rhythmic, melodic, and harmonic phrases and harmonic accompaniments within expanded forms (including introductions, transitions, and codas) that convey expressive intent.
- MU:Cr2.1.6b. Use standard and/or iconic notation and/or audio/video recording to document personal simple rhythmic phrases, melodic phrases, and two-chord harmonic musical ideas.
- MU:Cr3.1.8a. Evaluate their own work by selecting and applying criteria including appropriate application of compositional techniques, style, form, and use of sound sources.
- MU:Cr3.1.8b. Describe the rationale for refining works by explaining the choices, based on evaluation criteria.
- MU:Cr3.2.8a. Present the final version of their documented personal composition, song, or arrangement, using craftsmanship and originality to demonstrate the application of compositional techniques for creating unity and variety, tension and release, and balance to convey expressive intent.
- MU:Re7.2.6a. Describe how the elements of music and expressive qualities relate to the structure of the pieces.
- MU:Re8.1.6a. Describe a personal interpretation of how creators' and performers' application of the elements of music and expressive qualities, within genres and cultural and historical context, convey expressive intent.
- MU:Re9.1.8a. Apply appropriate personally developed criteria to evaluate musical works or performances.
- MU:Cn10.0.6a. Describe how interests, knowledge, and skills relate to personal choices and intent when creating, performing, and responding to music.

Materials

- A *Color Me Moody Sketchpage* for each composing team
- Paint chips in a variety of colors
- A variety of acoustic and digital instruments
- Recording from Ken Nordine's *Colors*, "Orange" and "Olive" are good examples
- A copy of the *Critical Reflections Guide* for each composer (see appendix B)

Project Time

- It will take approximately 50 minutes to complete.

DISCUSSION QUESTIONS TO DEVELOP COMPOSITIONAL CAPACITIES

? Feelingful Intention—How might we describe (color's) character, mood, or attitude? (For example, "How might we describe Indigo's character, mood, or attitude?")
? Musical Expressivity—What would it feel like to be (color)? Would (color) have more motion or stasis? What would be the quality of that? What would unify (color) and what would create variety? Is (color) about a particular type of sound? Is silence ever important to (color)? Are there times when (color) feels tension? How is that tension released? Is (color) a stable or unstable character?
? Artistic Craftsmanship—What types of sounds might best evoke the idea of (color)?

SEQUENCE OF ACTIVITIES

Phase 1—Listening

- As a class, critically listen to one or two of Ken Nordine's *Color* pieces. Play each piece twice. On the first listening, ask students to pay close attention to the text. What is happening in the poem? Try to draw out the term "personification."
- For the second listening, focus students on what is happening in the music. Does the music match the text in mood and character, offer additional insight into the character's mood or feelings, or suggest how others think about the character, or something else? How is this accomplished? (MU:Re8.1.6a)

Phase 2—Creating Poetry and Music to Personify Color

- Introduce today's project in which students will work in small groups to personify a color. Review with students what "personification" means. Ask for examples of personification by holding up objects from around the classroom while students offer a line or two that the object might say or that might be said about the object as if it were a person.
- Divide the class into small groups. Teams of five work well for this project, as one student will become the narrator and others will play instruments.
- Distribute the project *Sketchpage* to each team and allow them to select a paint chip to be their focus. Tell students that they do not need to use the color name provided on the paint chip and that they may rename their color if they wish.
- Encourage students to brainstorm ideas about their color and create their poem before they try to compose their musical accompaniments. (MU:Cr1.1.8a)
- Provide students with a selection of staff papers found in the appendices of this text. Students may use whatever notation system they find most helpful in capturing their musical ideas. Some students may forego notation and rely on memory. (MU:Cr2.1.6b)

Phase 3—Sharing and Discussion

- Each team should have an opportunity to perform their work for the class. Encourage narrators read with a dramatic flair representative of their color. (MU:Cr3.2.8a)
- As audience members listen to each performance, they should be ready to identify examples of personification in the text as well as compositional ideas that contributed to the drama of the work. (MU:Re7.2.6a)

Phase 4—Reflection and Self-Assessment

- Following the performance, students should engage in thinking critically about their learning, their compositional processes, and their musical products.
- After hearing the audiences' impressions of the work, prompt the composers to identify a few of their favorite spots in the piece. What compositional techniques (sounds) did they use? How did those sounds invite the experience of the MUSTS? What feeling or mood were they trying to capture? (MU:Cr3.1.8a)
- The *Critical Reflections Guide* located in the appendix can serve as a useful tool for fostering this important skill. (MU:Re9.1.8a; MU:Cr3.1.8b; MU:Cn10.0.6a)

Optional Extension

This project can be used to create longer works in a few different ways:

- Pieces could be strung together, without narration, as a rondo or in another form.
- Teams could be provided with two colors to use as inspiration for a conversation-styled work. The colors should be dramatic opposites and larger teams might be needed to perform these works.
- Color chips could be used to create mood pieces. Have students sequence eight to ten color chips and then improvise or compose a piece that moves through all the moods implied by the colors. Shifts might be gradual or abrupt.

Color Me Moody

Per·son·i·fi·ca·tion: Giving human characteristics and qualities to something non-human.

- Groups: 1 narrator and 4 singers/players
- Write an 8 line poem personifying your color. Poem should be written in 3rd person. Use the color's name as it was used in the listening models.
- Use acoustic or digital instruments for composing musical accompaniment
- Total writing and composing time: 15 minutes.
- Pieces will be performed today!

Brainstorm a few descriptive words that capture the character of your color.

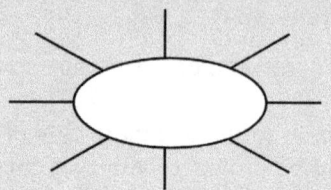

TITLE:		
Poem Line 1:		
Feelingful Intention:	Musical Expressivity (M.U.S.T.S.)	Artistic Craftsmanship:
Poem Line 2:		
FI:	ME:	AC:
Poem Line 3:		
FI:	ME:	AC:
Poem Line 4:		
FI:	ME:	AC:
Poem Line 5:		
FI:	ME:	AC:
Poem Line 6:		
FI:	ME:	AC:
Poem Line 7:		
FI:	ME:	AC:
Poem Line 8:		
FI:	ME:	AC:

Source: Created by Michele Kaschub and Janice P. Smith.

PROJECTS FOR INTERMEDIATE COMPOSERS

Chapter 13

Haiku Opera

Intermediate Level

Composition Strand: Songwriting

About this Project

The combining of haiku and grand theater into "Haiku Opera" invites composers to explore the processes of imagining and creating a large-scale musical form, but in an accessible miniature.

hai·ku li·bret·to
min·i·a·tur·ist mus·ic
ti·ny op·e·ra

While all operas present a story of some kind, musical traditions, forms, and singing styles vary around the world. Each opera tends to feature characteristics unique to its point of origin. This lesson is primarily concerned with opera of Western art traditions. However, the lesson is malleable in that examples of opera can be drawn from any tradition to serve as models for this project. Focusing on Chinese opera in the modeling process, for example, will likely result in final products sounding more like Chinese opera than other styles.

National Arts Standards for Music

Through this lesson, students will have the opportunity to:

- MU:Cr2.1.8a. Select, organize, and document personal musical ideas for arrangements, songs, and compositions within expanded forms that demonstrate tension and release, unity and variety, balance, and convey expressive intent.
- MU:Cr3.1.8a. Evaluate their own work by selecting and applying criteria including appropriate application of compositional techniques, style, form, and use of sound sources.
- MU:Cr3.1.8b. Describe the rationale for refining works by explaining the choices, based on evaluation criteria.
- MU:Cr3.2.8a. Present the final version of their documented personal composition, song, or arrangement, using craftsmanship and originality to demonstrate the application of compositional techniques for creating unity and variety, tension and release, and balance to convey expressive intent.
- MU:Re7.2.6a. Describe how the elements of music and expressive qualities relate to the structure of the pieces.
- MU:Re7.2.7a. Classify and explain how the elements of music and expressive qualities relate to the structure of contrasting pieces.
- MU:Re7.2.8a. Compare how the elements of music and expressive qualities relate to the structure within programs of music.

- MU:Re8.1.6a. Describe a personal interpretation of how creators' and performers' application of the elements of music and expressive qualities, within genres and cultural and historical context, convey expressive intent.
- MU:Re9.1.8a. Apply appropriate personally developed criteria to evaluate musical works or performances.
- MU:Cn10.0.7a. Demonstrate how interests, knowledge, and skills relate to personal choices and intent when creating, performing, and responding to music.

Materials

- A set of *Sketchpages* for each composer
- A vast collection of opera songs can be found at https://www.opera-arias.com. Clips vary with some video, some audio, some staged opera, and some opera excerpts performed in concert settings. This site can be searched by opera, composer, voice part, and configuration (solo, trio, chorus, etc.).
- Instruments or software for creating instrumental accompaniments
- Recording devices, if a record of the performances is desired
- A *Critical Reflection Guide* for each composer (see appendix B)

Project Time

This project may be approached in several different ways based on available class time and the team/compositional skills of the composers. Options include:

1. Whole class creating one story with small groups composing one song to fit into the class project. The product will be one opera. This will take four to five class sessions to complete.
2. Whole class creating one story and each small group composing multiple songs to tell the story from their perspective. The product will be multiple operas based on one story. This will take six to eight classes to complete.
3. Small groups creating their own stories and composing multiple songs. The product will be several different operas. This will take six to eight classes to complete.
4. Cultural variation: Use the group framework described in #2 or #3, but have students listen to opera from different traditions. For example, listening to Italian opera or Chinese opera as conceptual models may lead to different creative choices.

DISCUSSION QUESTIONS TO DEVELOP COMPOSITIONAL CAPACITIES

? Feelingful Intention—What is the overall mood of the opera? What is the emotional journey of the characters? What is the feelingful intent behind each song?

? Musical Expressivity—For each of the pieces within the opera, which of the MUSTS will be most important in inviting the desired emotional response?

? Artistic Craftsmanship—What tools and techniques of composition are best suited for shaping each song within the opera? What musical ideas or choices will serve to unite the separate songs into a musical whole?

SEQUENCE OF ACTIVITIES

Phase I—Setting the Creative Challenge

Present and discuss the terms *haiku* and *opera* with the class to familiarize students with the two art forms that will be combined in this project.

- What is *haiku*? Haiku is a form of Japanese poetic verse. When written in English, it usually consists of three unrhymed lines using 5, 7, and 5 syllables respectively. Haiku often evokes an image or pair two opposing images to capture a specific moment in time. Early haiku were used to set the scene for a larger verse to follow. As such, haiku often featured seasonal imagery. Over time, haiku became an independent form of verse but continued to offer juxtaposed ideas, inviting contemplation with strong imagery and few words.
- As a class, write a haiku. Then, have students write a haiku on their own. Take time to hear a few examples or have students pair and share their writing. This activity will help students gain confidence in their ability to create a libretto using this poetic form.
- Next, consider opera. Opera, unlike haiku, is anything but concise. Rather, an opera is a large-scale dramatic story told through the combination of art, words, music, theater, and dance. Operatic works are typically sung throughout and use music to make myths, fables, and tales more magical, more exciting, more expansive, and rarely believable. Opera is often about more, more, and more! The songs that deliver these stories typically fit into one of four categories: *recitative* (short and speech-like); *aria* (vocal solos that are expansive in range and delivered with great emotion); *ensemble* (duets, trios, quartets, and more, but typically the main characters each singing their own melody); and *chorus* (a group singing together in unison or parts).
- Gather an example of each opera song type described above. Play each one for the class and challenge students to identify to which category it belongs. Take time to note some of the key features as these observations will provide ideas for future composing. (MU:Re7.2.7a)
- Introduce the creative challenge of creating a "Haiku Opera" which will be presented in a single act. Here is an example that can be shared with students to help them understand that ideas do not need to be overly complex to be affective. This example centers on a Romeo & Juliet-type scenario.

Source: Created by Michele Kaschub and Janice P. Smith.

Phase II—Creating the Story

- Now that students have a basic understanding of both haiku structure and operatic styles, they should begin to plan their stories. Students may modify and recast existing stories. If using this approach, work with your school librarian or literature teachers to create a list of stories, fables, and myths suitable for the project. Conversely, the creation of original story material can deepen student investment in the project. The two approaches are likely to take about the same amount.

- Distribute the *Creating the Story Sketchpage* and briefly review its contents before setting students to work.
- When students have finished making these decisions about their opera story, have them present their ideas to you. Help them resolve any inconsistencies or places where you think they may have unclear story ideas. Try to ask questions rather than state opinions as you guide them to critically examine their work.

Phase III—Song List, Libretto, and Music

- As each team completes their initial story plan review with you, give them the *Building a Song List Sketchpage*. As you do this, suggest to students that they limit their list to six to eight songs. As most songs are likely to be 30–60 seconds in length, this will result in a 5- to 10-minute opera once the overture and finale bookend the project.
- When teams have completed creating their song list, give them copies of the *Writing the Libretto and Planning Songs* and the *Composing Songs Sketchpages* to guide their process. (MU:Cr2.1.8a)
- Composing processes vary from person to person and team to team. While it is easiest for you to control the workflow of the project by insisting that the libretto be finished before students begin writing music, some students may prefer to write the libretto for one song and create its music immediately or even at the same time. Both approaches are appropriate as long as the "big picture story" remains constant. If students are using staff paper, make a pile available. If students are working in digital audio workstations, now is the time to make sure they know the essential functions of the software they will be using.
- Given that this is a multilayered project, it will be beneficial for you to check progress. Students might offer daily report at the end of class by simply stating how many songs they are creating, how many have written lyrics, and how many have composed music. Stress the importance of "Save Often!"

Phase IV—Composers' Circle

- Once students have a few songs fully composed, facilitate a Composers' Circle in which each composer or team shares one song from their haiku opera. (MU:Cr3.2.8a)
- The composer/team should provide a synopsis of the story, explain where the selected song is situated in the opera, and ask their classmates for any specific feedback they may wish to receive. (MU:Re7.2.6a; MU:Re8.1.6a)
- The Composers' Circle provides a teaching opportunity as you may hear moments of compositional struggling where composers would benefit from listening to some additional opera recordings. If you encourage students to do some additional listening, work with them to help them hear the tools and techniques that may be of use in addressing their particular compositional challenges.

Phase V—Arranging the Overture and the Finale

- Take a few minutes to introduce the entire class to the instrumental pieces commonly associated with staging an opera. Students already may be familiar with overtures and finales as they are used in cinema. These pieces may have considerable overlap with their operatic peers. For example, *Mary Poppins Returns* (2018) opens with an overture much like that of an opera in that it:
  - features the catchiest songs of the show woven together to hint at the emotional journey that will unfold in the story.
  - presents the selected song themes in the order in which they will be featured in the show. (Note: This practice is a stylistic choice and some composers find it more affective to alter song order.)
  - it is performed before the movie begins/curtain rises and not part of the film or stage action.
- Distribute the *Overture and Finale Sketchpages*. As they begin to think about the overture, invite students to revisit their song lists with these questions in mind:
  - Which of the songs in our opera have strong hooks—these very short melodic or rhythmic ideas that stick in your ear?

- What tune is the audience going to be humming after the show?
- Are there any melodic or rhythmic ideas that are used in multiple songs? (MU:Re7.2.8a)
• Instruct the students to take these fragments and explore different ways that they might fit together. For example, the ideas could be strung one after another or it may be possible to overlap two or more ideas and have them performed at the same time. Encourage experimentation. (MU:Cr2.1.8a)
• When students move on to the finale, they can pursue three options:
  - Use material from the last song or most climatic song and state it in a slightly different manner (most common).
  - Repeat the overture (easiest and used sometimes).
  - Create completely new music (least common). (MU:Re7.2.8a)
• Remind students that the overture and the finale may be longer than some of their songs.

Phase VI—Rehearse and Perform

Students have likely been singing and playing their songs as they composed them. While this activity provides a level of rehearsal, students will need some additional time to practice running their show from start to finish.

• To stage or not to stage? Staging opera, even miniature opera, takes a fair amount of time. This could be time very well spent in helping students understand more of what is required of musicians who bring stories to life through drama and song. However, staging is not absolutely necessary. Opera can also be "concertized"—performed without staging. Students may wish to wear hats or simple masks to enhance a concertized performance. (MU:Cr3.2.8a)
• For a full immersion approach, consider presenting the student operas in either staged or concertized version to an audience beyond the classroom. (MU:Cr3.2.8a)

Phase VII—Reflection and Self-Assessment

• Following the performance, engage students in thinking critically about their learning, their compositional processes, and their musical products. The *Critical Reflection Guide* located in the appendix can serve as a useful tool for fostering this important skill. (MU:Cr3.1.8a, MU:Cr3.1.8b, MU:Re9.1.8a; MU:Cn10.0.7a)

Optional Extensions

• Take time to fully stage the opera. This works best for single operas created by the whole class working together or working with a song list distributed across several composing groups or teams. All students should have a role in staging the opera. Think about who will be singers, instrumentalists, conductors, stage directors, property master, costume design, lighting, makeup, program design, and so on.
• From the outset of the process, plan the opera to be delivered by puppets. Shadow puppetry allows performers to remain somewhat anonymous, or at least hidden, behind a screen. Some middle school students will prefer this gentler entry into the world of stagecraft. There are numerous books detailing how to create shadow puppets, and puppetry may provide an opportunity for collaboration with art educators. Note: This would be a wonderful opportunity for interdisciplinary arts work as students might explore Chinese Shadow Puppetry and Chinese Opera at the same time.
• This show can also be produced with cartoon images created in a slideshow presentation. Minimal animations are needed to deliver scenes as songs are very brief.

Creating a Story in 7 Steps

Step 1: Stories often begin in the mind of the writer with a memory of person, special place, a problem, a lingering fear.	What is your memory story?
Step 2: Think about quirky, inspiring, interesting, brainy, romantic, quiet, or influential people you know. Swap around their genders, ages, habits, personality traits, etc. Provide a quick description of the character. What is their role (queen, lawyer, gardener, butterfly catcher, baseball player, business person, etc.)?	Who will that main character be?
Step 3: Engaging stories often start with the main character immediately in terrible trouble.	What trouble will your main character get into? What is the problem they face?
Step 4: Operas often feature stories where everything the main character does to get out of trouble ends up making the trouble worse.	What does your character try and how does it make the situation worse?
Step 5: It is probably best in this short project to have just 2 or 3 characters.	Who are the other characters in your opera? How do they help or hinder the main character?
Step 6: About three-quarters of the way through the opera, it should seem like all hope is lost.	Which character is going to help the audience fear the worst or find hope?
Step 7: Often the resolution of the story is the result of the main character realizing that they have learned something along the way that will help them.	What has the main character learned? How will this situation be resolved?

CHECK POINT

Read through your story. Does it make sense? Does one event lead to the next in a logical manner?

Source: Created by Michele Kaschub and Janice P. Smith.

Building a Song List

How many songs will it take to deliver the story? Try to limit the song list to 6-8 songs. Describe your songs here.

Song	Character name	sings about	an idea, person, place, or thing.
1		sings about	
2		sings about	
3		sings about	
4		sings about	
5		sings about	
6		sings about	
7		sings about	
8		sings about	

Additional thoughts or questions to ask about this song list:

Source: Created by Michele Kaschub and Janice P. Smith.

Writing the Libretto & Planning Songs

The words of an opera are called the *libretto*. When a character sings words that tell part of the story, the libretto style is *narrative*. If song lines are exchanged, the libretto is *conversational*. If the chorus offers an opinion, the libretto is *commentative*. A mix of these styles creates interest.

For this project, the libretto will be written in *haiku*. Haiku is a form of Japanese poetry. When written in English, it usually consists of three unrhymed lines using a 5, 7, and 5 syllables. Haiku features strong imagery to capture a specific moment in time or presents two opposing ideas to invite people to think deeply about how things are related.

Syllables refer to the sounds within a word. "Word" has one syllable, "music" has two, and so on. If you are not sure about how many syllables are in a word you want to use, look it up. A dictionary will show the word broken into its parts like this: syl·la·ble.)

As you write the libretto for each song, take a few moments to consider how the music needs to sound to convey the emotional tone that will advance the story. Note your plan for each capacity in the box beside the libretto.

Song 1 Title: _____

Character(s)/Chorus: _____

Line 1 ____ ____ ____ ____ ____

Line 2 ____ ____ ____ ____ ____ ____ ____

Line 3 ____ ____ ____ ____ ____

What is the feelingful intention for this song?

Which of the musical expressivities (M.U.S.T.S.) will be most important for inviting the desired response?

What artistic craftsmanship techniques are best suited for this particular song?

Song 2 Title: _____

Character(s)/Chorus: _____

Line 1 ____ ____ ____ ____ ____

Line 2 ____ ____ ____ ____ ____ ____ ____

Line 3 ____ ____ ____ ____ ____

What is the feelingful intention for this song?

Which of the musical expressivities (M.U.S.T.S.) will be most important for inviting the desired response?

What artistic craftsmanship techniques are best suited for this particular song?

Source: Created by Michele Kaschub and Janice P. Smith.

Song 3 Title: _____ Character(s)/Chorus:_____ Line 1 ___ ___ ___ ___ ___ Line 2 ___ ___ ___ ___ ___ ___ ___ Line 3 ___ ___ ___ ___ ___	What is the feelingful intention for this song? Which of the musical expressivities (M.U.S.T.S.) will be most important for inviting the desired response? What artistic craftsmanship techniques are best suited for this particular song?
Song 4 Title: _____ Character(s)/Chorus:_____ Line 1 ___ ___ ___ ___ ___ Line 2 ___ ___ ___ ___ ___ ___ ___ Line 3 ___ ___ ___ ___ ___	What is the feelingful intention for this song? Which of the musical expressivities (M.U.S.T.S.) will be most important for inviting the desired response? What artistic craftsmanship techniques are best suited for this particular song?
Song 5 Title: _____ Character(s)/Chorus:_____ Line 1 ___ ___ ___ ___ ___ Line 2 ___ ___ ___ ___ ___ ___ ___ Line 3 ___ ___ ___ ___ ___	What is the feelingful intention for this song? Which of the musical expressivities (M.U.S.T.S.) will be most important for inviting the desired response? What artistic craftsmanship techniques are best suited for this particular song?
Song 6 Title: _____ Character(s)/Chorus:_____ Line 1 ___ ___ ___ ___ ___ Line 2 ___ ___ ___ ___ ___ ___ ___ Line 3 ___ ___ ___ ___ ___	What is the feelingful intention for this song? Which of the musical expressivities (M.U.S.T.S.) will be most important for inviting the desired response? What artistic craftsmanship techniques are best suited for this particular song?

Composing Songs

1. Review your song lyrics.

2. Consider your feelingful intention, musical expressivities, and artistic craftsmanship notes.

3. Close your eyes and imagine the character who will sing this song on a stage. What do you hear? Jot down or record any ideas that come to mind.

4. Start exploring musical ideas. Some composer begin by singing melodies, other play chords, and others create accompaniments and then sing over them to "find the song". Use whatever approach works best for you.

What type of song do you need?

- *Recitative* – short and speech-like; good for quickly delivering information
- *Aria* – vocal solo; shares information, delivered with great dramatic emotion
- *Ensemble* – duets, trios, quartets, etc. of main characters; each sings their own melody in aria-like fashion; they may take turns or sing at the same time
- *Chorus* – not main characters; group singing in unison or parts

Source: Created by Michele Kaschub and Janice P. Smith.

Composing the Overture

An *overture* is an instrumental piece that is performed before the stage action begins. Overtures are created by weaving together excerpts of the songs from the show. They usually feature the catchiest songs woven together to hint at the emotional journey that will unfold in the story. The excerpts are usually presented in show order, but they do not have to be.

1. The first task in composing an overture is to compose all the songs in the show. You've done this!

2. The next step is to find the best musical ideas in all of that work. As you shop your song list for overture ideas, consider these questions:
   - Which of the songs has the strongest *hook* – a very short melody or rhythmic idea that sticks in your ear? Another way to think about this is: What tune do you think the audience will hum/sing/whistle after the show?
   - What is the most important song in the show?
   - Are there any melodic or rhythmic ideas that appear in multiple songs?
   - If many of the songs have a similar tempo or mood, which one provides contrast?

3. Build your overture plan. Briefly name or describe your chosen excerpts here. Limit yourself to 3 – 6 ideas. If you are working with staff paper, draw all of your excerpts on a new sheet. If you are working in a digital-audio workspace, open a new project file and copy and paste your chosen excerpts into it.

4. Once you have organized your excerpts, explore playing them in different ways. Listen to them played one after another, trying overlapping them or stacking them on top of each other, add a bass line, use one of them as a bass line, etc. Experiment until you find just the right combination and placement for the excerpts. Finally, add a few new musical ideas around these one to complete the overture.

Source: Created by Michele Kaschub and Janice P. Smith.

Composing the Finale

1. After all that drama, it is important to provide some musical closure to the opera experience. The finale does just that. It is a reinforcement of how the story turned out. If the story has a happy ending, the finale is usually equally upbeat. Stories ending with a darker twist often echo those emotions in the final notes.

2. Composer usually choose one of three ways to present the closing instrumental piece. They:
   - Use material from the last song or most climatic song and state it in a slightly different manner (most common).
   - Repeat the overture (easiest and used sometimes).
   - Create completely new music (least common).

3. Decide which of these approaches seems best suited to your story line and also fits well with the music you have already written.

Questions about the Finale	The Plan for the Finale
What is the feelingful intention of the Finale?	
Which of the M.U.S.T.S. will be important in making this final impression on the audience?	
What compositional techniques will you use to craft the finale?	
Are there melodic ideas, rhythmic figures, or instrumentation from earlier in the show that will be used as it ends?	
Will you repeat music from earlier in the show? If so, does this music already carry the feelingful intention need for the finale? Must it be altered in some way? How will you do this?	
Is new music needed? Why?	
How will you make sure that new music connects with the rest of the show?	

Source: Created by Michele Kaschub and Janice P. Smith.

Chapter 14

One Scene, Many Interpretations

Intermediate Level

Composition Strand: Film Scoring

About this Project

This project invites students to create music for a particular scene and then hone their critical-thinking skills by comparing and contrasting their work with those of other composers creating music for the same scene. Using the compositional capacities as a framework for discussion, students listen, view, and comment on their own work as well as the work of others.

National Arts Standards for Music

This lesson presents students with an opportunity to:

- MU:Cr1.1.8a. Generate rhythmic, melodic, and harmonic phrases and harmonic accompaniments within expanded forms (including introductions, transitions, and codas) that convey expressive intent.
- MU:Cr2.1.8a. Select, organize, and document personal musical ideas for arrangements, songs, and compositions within expanded forms that demonstrate tension and release, unity and variety, balance, and convey expressive intent.
- MU:Cr3.1.8a. Evaluate their own work by selecting and applying criteria including appropriate application of compositional techniques, style, form, and use of sound sources.
- MU:Cr3.1.8b. Describe the rationale for refining works by explaining the choices, based on evaluation criteria.
- MU:Re9.1.8a. Apply appropriate personally developed criteria to evaluate musical works or performances.
- MU:Cn11.0.7a. Demonstrate understanding of relationships between music and the other arts, other disciplines, varied contexts, and daily life.

Materials

- Copies of all *Sketchpages* with additional copies of the timeline and staff paper pages for students to use as needed (see appendices)
- Instruments, music notation software or movie production software with sound-production capabilities
- A specific scene from a movie which could be interpreted in various ways
- A copy of the *Critical Reflection Guide* for each composer (see appendix B)

Project Time

- It will take approximately 30 minutes to compose the music for the scene and then at least 10 minutes per composition to discuss and review.

DISCUSSION QUESTIONS TO DEVELOP COMPOSITIONAL CAPACITIES

? Feelingful Intention—What might the audience feel when viewing this scene? Which of these feelings do you think are best suited to this scene? Why? Is there any point at which contrasting feelings occur? Are these changes in feeling abrupt or more smoothly transitioned?

? Musical Expressivity—How will the use of music enhance the feeling of the scene? What might film music supporting the feeling(s) identified for this scene sound like? Does this scene require a musical theme? Which of the MUSTS will be most important in giving rise to this feeling? Does the sense of motion change in the scene? What will unify the music for this scene? Is there any point of instability in the scene? How will the music reflect that? Where is the height of the tension in the scene? Will the music enhance or contrast with that tension? What should the overall sound concept for this scene be?

? Artistic Craftsmanship—How might the music reflect the dramatic arc of the scene? What instruments or other sound sources will be used? How will the sounds be organized and performed with the film? Can we make our film score even more expressive? How?

SEQUENCE OF ACTIVITIES

Phase 1—Teacher Preparation

- Select a scene from a film to use for this activity. Alternatively, select three to five scenes and allow the class to vote to determine which will be used. Teacher selection is more efficient; student voting may lead to more expressive work and a greater sense of ownership in the project.
- Movie clips or short films can be found in a number of places. A resource with everything from old advertisements to independent shorts to cartoons is *archive.org*. Another option is YouTube. Using silent movies such as *Le Manoir du Diable* (the first horror movie) or the films of Charlie Chaplin are other options.
- Criteria for selection:
  ○ The scene should be unfamiliar to the students. Avoid recent films that they might have seen and from which they might be able to recall the music.
  ○ The scene should be fairly short: 2–3 minutes is about right in most cases.
- The clip should be stripped of the existing sound. This can be done in most movie editing software. Alternatively, the teacher can play the clip for the whole class with the sound turned off.

Phase 2—Composition Time

- Play the chosen film clip for the class and ask them to imagine the music. After the film finishes, *do not* discuss what they have imagined (as this will influence peers and create a shared vision while the goal of this lesson is to explore different musical interpretations of the scene). (MU:Cr1.18a)
- Divide the class into small groups or pairs. If students are working with a computer, pairs or trios with headphones will work best. If using acoustic sound sources or a mixture of both, students can be encouraged to work quietly. (MU:Cr2.1.8a)
- Distribute the *Sketchpage* and play or have the students play the clip again. Direct students to work through *Sketchpages*. The final *Sketchpage* provides space for students to notate simple ideas. If students are working with a large number of instruments they may need multi-stave paper (see appendix). If students are creating their film scores using software, they will not need to notate. Students may be asked to take screen shots of musical material that they create which provides a "snapshot" of their best work. These snapshots could provide a visual cue for reflective writing about what they learned as they created their film scores. (MU:Cr2.1.8a)
- Allow the groups about 15 minutes to work, adjusting the time as necessary to allow groups to complete their work.

Phase 3—Sharing and Discussion

- Have each team take turns sharing their work with the class. (MU:Cr3.2.8a) Based on your observations of their progress as they worked, try to start with two quite contrasting scores. Have the composers discuss their artistic choices based on their *Sketchpages.* (MU:Cr3.1.8b)
- Conclude the discussion by emphasizing the multiplicity of possible artistic visions and why some may be more effective than others by emphasizing the ideas of imagining in sound and the use of the MUSTS to evoke their feelingful intentions.

Phase 4—Reflection and Self-Assessment

- Have the students complete the *Critical Reflection Guide* located in the appendix. (MU:Cr3.1.8a, MU:Cr3.1.8b, MU:Re9.1.8a, MU:Cn10.0.7a)

Optional Extension

This project can be repeated with a different film clip after the class views and discusses this project. Composers often garner ideas from this that they use in future compositions. Another extension possibility is for students to create their own short movies and compose the music and create sound effects needed to present the story cinematically.

One Scene, Many Interpretations

Feelingful Intention
- List some possibilities for what the audience could feel when viewing this scene?
- Which one do we wish to use?
- Is there any point at which a contrasting feeling occurs?

Musical Expressivity
- How will music enhance the feeling of the scene?
- Which of the M.U.S.T.S. seem likely to be most important to give rise to this feeling?
    - Does the sense of motion change in the scene?
    - What will unify the music for this scene?
    - Is there any point of instability in the scene?
    - Where is the height of the tension in the scene? Will the music enhance or contrast with that tension?
    - What should the overall sound of this scene be?
- Does this scene require a theme?

Artistic Craftsmanship
- How will our music reflect the dramatic arc of the scene?
- What instruments or other sound sources will be used?
- How will the sounds be organized and performed with the film?
- Can we make our score even more expressive? How?

Source: Created by Michele Kaschub and Janice P. Smith.

Film Score Blueprint

Create a musical blueprint for your scene using this timeline. Note important events by marking the minute/second they occur. Add a few words of description to remind you what is happening at each point. Indicate feelingful intentions, musical expressivities (MUSTS) and craftsmanship ideas beside these notes. Remember to consider how the music will sound between events, too. If your scene is long or action heavy, you may need addition blueprint sheets to make your plan.

0/0

Source: Created by Michele Kaschub and Janice P. Smith.

MOVIE MUSIC

Frame 1
- Movie frame start time:
- Feelingful intention:
- Musical expressivity:
- Artistic craftsmanship:

Frame 2
- Movie frame start time:
- Feelingful intention:
- Musical expressivity:
- Artistic craftsmanship:

Frame 3
- Movie frame start time:
- Feelingful intention:
- Musical expressivity:
- Artistic craftsmanship:

Frame 4
- Movie frame start time:
- Feelingful intention:
- Musical expressivity:
- Artistic craftsmanship:

Source: Created by Michele Kaschub and Janice P. Smith.

Chapter 15

Upcycled Music

Intermediate Level

Composition Strand: Instrumental Music

About this Project

Long before the notion of "being green" came into existence, composers practiced a form of music recycling by using excerpts of their own pieces, and sometimes the music of others, to make quick work of creating new pieces. In this project, composers will use upcycling—the process of transforming old items or discarded materials into new products of better quality and value—to invent an instrument and a composition with a little twenty-first-century music repurposing.

National Arts Standards for Music

This lesson presents students with an opportunity to:

- MU:Cr1.1.8a. Generate rhythmic, melodic, and harmonic phrases and harmonic accompaniments within expanded forms (including introductions, transitions, and codas) that convey expressive intent.
- MU:Cr2.1.7a. Select, organize, develop, and document personal musical ideas for arrangements, songs, and compositions within AB, ABA, or theme and variation forms that demonstrate unity and variety and convey expressive intent.
- MU:Cr3.1.8a. Evaluate their own work by selecting and applying criteria including appropriate application of compositional techniques, style, form, and use of sound sources.
- MU:Cr3.1.8b. Describe the rationale for refining works by explaining the choices, based on evaluation criteria.
- MU:Cr3.2.8a. Present the final version of their documented personal composition, song, or arrangement, using craftsmanship and originality to demonstrate the application of compositional techniques for creating unity and variety, tension and release, and balance to convey expressive intent.
- MU:Re7.1.6a. Select or choose music to listen to and explain the connections to specific interests or experiences for a specific purpose.
- MU:Re7.1.7a. Select or choose contrasting music to listen to and compare the connections to specific interests or experiences for a specific purpose.
- MU:Re8.1.6a. Describe a personal interpretation of how creators' and performers' application of the elements of music and expressive qualities, within genres and cultural and historical context, convey expressive intent.
- MU:Re9.1.8a. Apply appropriate personally developed criteria to evaluate musical works or performances.
- MU:Cn10.0.7a. Demonstrate how interests, knowledge, and skills relate to personal choices and intent when creating, performing, and responding to music.

Materials

- A set of project *Sketchpages* for each composer
- Access to a variety of notation papers mixed in traditional formats (see appendices)
- YouTube videos: "Making Musical Instruments Out of Garbage," https://www.youtube.com/watch?v=wKzflCztXd4; Paul Dresher Ensemble, http://www.dresherensemble.org/works/invented-musical-instruments/ or something similar
- Collection of recyclables such as tin cans, cardboard tubes, cardboard boxes, scrap wood and metal, string, wire, etc.
- Tools and accessories such as strong tape, glue, hot glue guns/glue sticks, small brads, nails and screws of several sizes, hammers, electric screwdrivers, and other small project tools will be needed if instrument construction occurs in class.
- A "musical clippings collection"—printed music cut into single lines of various lengths, from 1–2 beats to 3–4 measures.
- A *Critical Reflection Guide* for each composer (see appendix B)

Project Time

- Phase 1 will take about 20 minutes of in-class time. Research may also be completed outside of class if students have Internet access.
- Phase 2 may take place in class or outside of school. Instrument-building time will vary by complexity of instrument. One class period should be sufficient for most instruments; additional time could be utilized if more complex instruments are desirable.
- Students will need 15–20 minutes to explore the sound potentials of their instrument in Phase 3.
- The creation of a composition in Phase 4 will take approximately 30–45 minutes. Handwritten notation may be most accurate as students may need to invent symbols for the unique sounds that their instruments may make.
- Phase 5 involves performances of the newly composed works. Each student should have time to offer a brief "show and tell" about their instrument, introduce their piece, and invite and hear feedback from other composers. This will take 4–5 minutes per student.

DISCUSSION QUESTIONS TO DEVELOP COMPOSITIONAL CAPACITIES

? Feelingful Intention—Which feelingful qualities are most likely to result from the sounds that can be made on your instrument?
? Musical Expressivity—Given the nature of your instrument, which of the expressivities might be most prominent in your composition? How will this contribute to the overall effect of your composition?
? Artistic Craftsmanship—Which musical elements and compositional tools will allow you to maximize the expressive potentials of your instrument within your composition?

SEQUENCE OF ACTIVITIES

Phase 1—Instrument Research and Concept Drawing

- Open the class by inviting students to think about how musical instruments are invented. Who creates them? How are they built? Who is most likely the first composer and performer for a new instrument? (MU:Cn10.0.7a)
- Distribute *Sketchpage 1: Creative Sound Investigation*. Ask students to create a list of materials that instruments are built from and the types of sounds that invented instruments make as they watch a few YouTube videos on instrument invention. *Making Musical Instruments Out of Garbage* and the *Paul Dresher Ensemble* are good places to start. Students will be able to find others. (MU:Re7.1.7a)

Phase 2—Instrument Invention

Note: If all students have access to a range of recyclables at home, this portion of the project may be completed outside of school. If such access is not available to all, encourage students to bring recyclable items they wish to use and extras to be shared among classmates. The teacher may also amass a collection of recyclables (the cafeteria kitchen may be a good place to start) and make these available for students. If instrument building is to take place at school, set up a work area with all materials, tools, and equipment—including safety equipment like goggles, heavy gloves, mats for glue guns, and so on, needed for construction.

- Review safety procedures related to the tools available for instrument building. While some students will be familiar with hot glue guns, saws and wire cutters, others may have had little experience and would benefit from a simple demonstration and a few words of instruction. It may be possible to partner with colleagues from industrial technologies to present safety and other "how-to" information.
- Distribute *Sketchpage 2: Instrument Invention Planner* and encourage students to consider what materials are available. Students may need to handle and explore materials to develop an understanding of their sound potentials.
- Once students have completed the planning process outlined on the *Sketchpage*, review the plans and criteria, and ask question that will help students further refine their visions. Invite students to gather their materials and begin construction.
- Continuously walk the room and offer assistance as needed. Questions that lead students to solve problems themselves are best, but hands-on assistance may be needed at various points to assemble an instrument.

Phase 3—Exploring the Potentials of a New Instrument

- Distribute *Sketchpage 3: Explore Your Instrument* and review the compositional capacities as needed. (MU:Re7.1.6a; MU:Cr2.1.7a)
- Encourage students to take 15 minutes to purposefully explore what their instrument can do.
- For 5–10 minutes, partner students and encourage them to share what they have discovered about their instrument. Peers should be on the lookout for sounds that the instrument might make that the inventor may not have discovered. (MU:Cn10.0.7a)

Phase 4—Upcycled Music Composition

- Distribute *Sketchpage 4: Compose.*
- Invite students to work through the page as they plan compositions and work through the compositional process. Some students are likely to think of their pieces as having a beginning/middle/end organization. Students might also be introduced to the idea of creating multiple sonic events and ordering them within a time sequence. (MU:Cr1.1.8a)
- Regularly check in with students to make sure that all are making progress. If students seem stalled, ask questions to help them generate ideas or explore several options for solving their current problem.
- Miniature Composers' Circles, comprised of just three to four students, can be used to advance work if composers are struggling. Use of this technique will require a little additional work time, but peer feedback can offer new perspectives as composers work to discover the potentials of their newly created instrument. (MU:Cr3.1.8a; MU:Re8.1.6a)

Phase 5—Performance

- Performances of the newly composed works will occur in class. Each student should have time to present his or her newly invented instrument and model the sounds it can create. Students should give a brief introduction to their piece and offer a few words to guide listeners in understanding any special compositional goals or objectives. Audience members should be prepared to offer both compliment and constructive criticisms. (MU:Cr3.2.8a)

Phase 6—Reflection and Self-Assessment

- Following the performance, students should engage in thinking critically about their learning, their compositional processes, and their musical products. The *Critical Reflection Guide* found in the appendix can serve as a useful guide for fostering this important skill. (MU:Cr3.1.8a; MU:Cr3.1.8b; MU:Re9.1.8a; MU:Cn10.0.7a)

Optional Extension

Invite students to form several chamber music groups. Each group composes a work for its specific instruments and the class presents a recital of the "Upcycled Music for Chamber Ensemble." Students will want to consider each ensemble's instrumentation as the sound palettes they assemble will greatly influence the composition of their pieces.

UPCYCLE
Creative Sound Investigation

Where did you find the audio/video source for this instrument?				
What materials were used to build the instrument?				
Which instrument family would this instrument belong to? Why?				
What kind of sounds can the instrument make?				
How is the instrument played?				
What about this instrument works best?				

Source: Created by Michele Kaschub and Janice P. Smith with images from iStock/Credit: People Images.

Instrument Invention Planner

What materials and tools will be needed to build your instrument?

Invented instruments should be:
- able to make a minimum of five different sounds.
- playable by a single performer.
- able to project sound loud enough to hear within the classroom.

How will your instrument be put together?

What sounds will this instrument make?

Sketch your instrument here.

Source: Created by Michele Kaschub and Janice P. Smith.

Explore Your Instrument

FEELINGFUL INTENTION
Listen to the sounds that your instrument can make.

List a few descriptive words that capture how these sounds relate to different feelingful qualities.

Use these observations to inform your decisions as you craft your piece.

MUSICAL EXPRESSIVITY
Explore expressive potentials of your instrument.

Which of the M.U.S.T.S. are easiest to manipulate?

Are there any that are difficult to perform on the instrument?

Which of the expressivities will be most prominent in your composition?

ARTISTIC CRAFTSMANSHIP
Which musical elements and compositional tools will allow you to maximize the expressive potentials of your instrument within your composition?

Source: Created by Michele Kaschub and Janice P. Smith.

Consider your materials. Select a few fragments from the music clippings collection that you can upcycle in your new composition.

Optimize your creative energies. Without making any judgments about quality or how these ideas might fit into your piece, see how many new ideas can you make from these old ideas. Change pitches, rhythms, melodic contours, meter signatures, key signatures, dynamics, phrasings, articulations, etc. Sketch your ideas here or on a separate sheet of staff paper.

Manage your vision. Which of the new ideas will work on your instrument? Keep these. Set the rest aside. Arrange the best of the upcycled ideas into an order that you think has expressive impact. Place them here:

Produce new material. Draft a few original musical ideas to fill out the piece. If you are not sure how to notate an odd sound, invent your own symbols. This is usually easier to notate on paper. Test each idea to make sure it fits into the overall work. Assemble your piece one idea at a time. Remember, you can repeat ideas! Jot new ideas here or on a separate sheet of staff paper.

Options: Are you ready to finalize or do you need to revise? Finalize means creating the score while revision means returning to an earlier stage in the process. In either case, embrace the challenge! Your piece is coming together.

Score your work on paper or in a notation program. Complete final edits, double check expressive markings, and consider writing a few notes "from the composer" to explain any special or unique notation that you may have used.

Envision the performance. Practice your piece until you can play it with confidence. Enjoy sharing it with your audience.

Source: Created by Michele Kaschub and Janice P. Smith.

Chapter 16

Song Production

Intermediate Level

Composition Strand: Electronic Music and Digital Media

About this Project

When a songwriter turns their song over to a producer, the producer works to make the song sound the way they think it should sound to fit a specific performer and to be competitive within a particular commercial market (hip-hop, rhythm & blues, country, pop, electronic dance music, etc.). To do this, the producer may restructure the form of the song, weave in new ideas for vocals or instrumentals, improve the flow of lyrics, and consider alternate beats and tempos to capitalize on the raw material of the song.

In this project, students will exchange previously or newly written songs with a peer producer. The producer will rework the song material to fit a completely different market than the one intended by the songwriter. For example, if a songwriter submits a country song, the producer might reimagine it as hip-hop. This project allows students to experience releasing their songs "into the wild" for other artists to interpret.

Note: This lesson assumes familiarity with entry-level production software or apps. If students are new to these tools, be prepared to spend some time introducing basic skills.

National Arts Standards for Music

This lesson presents students with an opportunity to:

- MU:Cr2.1.8a. Select, organize, and document personal musical ideas for arrangements, songs, and compositions within expanded forms that demonstrate tension and release, unity and variety, balance, and convey expressive intent.
- MU:Cr3.1.8b. Describe the rationale for refining works by explaining the choices, based on evaluation criteria.
- MU:Cr3.2.8a. Present the final version of their documented personal composition, song, or arrangement, using craftsmanship and originality to demonstrate the application of compositional techniques for creating unity and variety, tension and release, and balance to convey expressive intent.
- MU:Re7.2.6b. Identify the context of music from a variety of genres, cultures, and historical periods.
- MU:Re8.1.6a. Describe a personal interpretation of how creators' and performers' application of the elements of music and expressive qualities, within genres and cultural and historical context, convey expressive intent.
- MU:Re8.1.7a. Describe a personal interpretation of contrasting works and explain how creators' and performers' application of the elements of music and expressive qualities, within genres, cultures, and historical periods, convey expressive intent.
- MU:Re9.1.8a. Apply appropriate personally developed criteria to evaluate musical works or performances.
- MU:Cn10.0.7a. Demonstrate how interests, knowledge, and skills relate to personal choices and intent when creating, performing, and responding to music.

Materials

- Copies of the *About My Song Sketchpage* for each songwriter or songwriting team
- Copies of the *Genre Reframe Sketchpage* and *Production Checklist* for each producer or production team
- Students will need a song that they have previously composed. If they do not have this, students will need to compose a new song for this project. The *Songwriter's Workshop* project in this text offers guidance for creating original songs.
- Access to a digital audio workstation (DAW). ProTools, Logic Pro, Ableton, Cubase, and FL Studio are common DAWs for production. Production work can also be accomplished with entry-level programs like GarageBand and Acoustica Mix-craft. These programs are available for both computers and smart devices. Additionally, apps like RemixLive and Figure are also good choices with free versions for students to use.
- A *Critical Reflection Guide* for each composer (see appendix B)

Project Time

- If working with already composed songs, this project can be completed in three to four work sessions. If students are writing a new song to set the stage for production work, add three to five class sessions.

DISCUSSION QUESTIONS TO DEVELOP COMPOSITIONAL CAPACITIES

? Feelingful Intention—What was the original feelingful intention for this song? How much of that intention will be carried into the new arrangement? Would a different feelingful intention be a better fit in the new genre?

? Musical Expressivity—Which of the MUSTS were most influential in the original songs? Will different MUSTS be emphasized in reframing the song?

? Artistic Craftsmanship—Which components of the original song should be maintained in the new version? What musical material needs to be added or discarded to cast the song in its new genre?

SEQUENCE OF ACTIVITIES

Phase 1—Meet the Producers

- Ask students to create a job description for a music producer. Allow them to work in pairs or trios and give them 5 minutes. Invite students to share answers and expand their definitions as needed. A summary description might include:
  - Works with an artist to develop their vision
  - Conceives of a music album
  - Hires songwriters
  - Employs a beat maker to create rhythmic backing tracks
  - Brings in singers and instrumentalists to perform music
  - Coaches the songwriter, performers, and others to increase the cohesiveness and quality of the song (or album)
  - Hires recording engineers to record the music
  - Contracts a mastering artist to adjust and refine the recorded version of the song
- Introduce the song production project letting students know that they will fill the roles of songwriter, performer, and producer as they share their own songs and produce a song composed by others in their class.

Phase 2—Song Material

- Decide whether this project will be undertaken by individual students or partners. Either format will work, but the choice does impact how students select the work they will share and produce songs.
- If composing new songs, see the guide for *A Songwriter's Workshop* in Chapter 8. Students will need to create and record their songs before taking the next steps in this project.
- If using songs previously composed and recorded by students, begin by having class establish criteria for song selection. Discuss how much song material needs to be offered to the producers. For example, will all song submissions need a refrain and a chorus as a minimum, or something else? (MU:Re9.1.8a)
- Once these types of questions have been addressed, students will need time to make their selections. If working individually, have students select the song they will present to the producers. If working in pairs, students may need to either create a new song together, use one they have previously composed together, or submit a song written by just one member of the team. It also may be possible to have the review of song material begin as a homework project and conclude with partners making final decisions in class.

Phase 3—The Pitch

- Distribute the *About My Song Sketchpage* and instruct songwriters prepare their pitch (presentation they will use to entice the producers to work on their song). (MU:Cr3.2.8a)
- Once the pitch sheets are complete, divide the students into two groups—songwriters and producers. Play a round of "speed meeting" giving songwriters and producers 5 minutes to meet and discuss each song.
- Meeting format: Each songwriter or team should present their song to two to three different producers. The producer or production team will then suggest an idea or two about how they might reimagine the song. (MU:Cr3.1.8b; MU:Re8.1.6a;) The songwriter(s) can then decide which producer or production team gets to work with their song OR the producer(s) can decide which song they want to work on. Have the class select a decision format before the meetings begin.

Phase 4—Reimagining the Song

- Place sound files for each piece in a location where producers can retrieve and upload them into the software or app they will use for this project.
- Present each producer or production team with a copy of the *Genre Reframe Sketchpage*. Quickly review what students are expected to do and set them to work. (MU:Cr2.1.8a; MU:Cr3.1.8b; MU:Re7.2.6b; MU:Re8.1.6a)
- As the Head of Production for My Class Records, you may ask producers to review their production plans with you before creating their new version of the song, or you can just let them get to it. A quick check-in and "yes, you are ready to move on" is reassuring for students who may be nervous about how they are doing with a new or unfamiliar task.

Phase 5—Producing the Song

- If students are working with unfamiliar DAWs, take time to introduce them to their tools. Students also will need to know the basic functions of the software or apps that they are using. Offer brief tutorials on creating a new file, adding and deleting tracks, locating sounds/loops, drag and drop features, recording acoustic tracks, editing track content (trimming, duplicating, cut and paste), and saving. It may be helpful to create a one-sheet guide offering quick steps for how to do each of these functions.
- Give each producer or team a *Production Checklist Sketchpage*. This will help producers consider their options as they begin to rework their songs. (MU:Cr2.1.8a)

Phase 6—Sharing and Discussion

- Invite producers to present their final products to the class. Each presentation should include listening to the original and the produced versions—but consider flipping the order from time to time. (MU:Cr3.2.8a)
- Ask students to consider:
  - How did the feelingful intention of the song change? Or, if it didn't, why did it stay the same when other features of the song changed?
  - Which of the MUSTS contributed most significantly to the alteration of the song?
  - What tools of production do you hear in the new version of the song? How do these production values contribute to the overall feel of the song? (MU:Re8.1.7a)

Phase 7—Reflection and Self-Assessment

- Have students complete the *Critical Reflections Guide* to document what they learned as they completed this project. (MU:Cr3.1.8a; MU:Cr3.1.8b; MU:Re9.1.8a; MU:Cn10.0.7a)

Optional Extension

- Divide the class into several production teams. Assign a specific genre to each team. Provide all teams with the same root song. Once songs are produced, listen to all and discuss how the song changes based on the genre in which it is situated.
- Hip-hop artists sometimes use classical music excerpts or quotes as loops within their work. Listen to a few classical selections and find a brief musical idea that might be used in this way. Tuck the classical idea into a new song.

About My Song

Lyrics	
	Song Title
	Genre
	Description
	What is the overall Feelingful Intention for this work?
	Which of the Musical Expressivities (M.U.S.T.S.) are most influential?
	What techniques of Artistic Craftsmanship will catch the listeners ear?
	Why I think you should produce my song:

The audio clip that I want to share with you begins (describe) and highlights how I (describe):

Source: Created by Michele Kaschub and Janice P. Smith with images from iStock/Credit: tostphoto.

Original Genre

- What genre is this song?

- What is the Feelingful Intention of this song?

- Which of the Musical Expressivities (M.U.S.T.S.) is most influential?

- Is there a particular tool of Artistic Craftsmanship that is memorable?

- What genre will be used to reframe this song?

- What will be the Feelingful Intention of the song in the new genre?

- Which of the Musical Expressivities (M.U.S.T.S.) will be most influential?

- What tools of Artistic Craftsmanship will be used to boost the memorability?

- Describe 5 things you imagine changing, adding to, or deleting from this song:

Genre Reframe

Source: Created by Michele Kaschub and Janice P. Smith with images from iStock/Credit: Kristine Semjonova.

Production Checklist

Production Actions

The following is a list of production actions that should be considered. Most of these actions may be approached in any order. The last item on the list is best reviewed near the end of the process.

☐ Sing through the original a few times so that you are comfortable singing the main ideas.

☐ Find a beat in that fits the genre you've identified for the song. Adjust the groove as needed. Consider beats that will loop.

☐ Add the keyboard or guitar chords. Is there a repeating pattern? Does it change in chorus or pre-chorus? Can these loop or do they vary?

☐ Work on the main vocal. Keep the primary line simple to leave room for additional vocals.

☐ Add vocal harmony, echoes, or commentary figures around the main line.

☐ Add a bass. Consider how the bass line adds punctuation to the beat track.

☐ Listen to the layers: high/forward/main vocal, low/background/bass/beat, middle ground/guitar/instrumental fills. Are all present? Are all balanced so that the important musical figures are easy to hear?

☐ Check sound levels for each track. Listen several times and adjust balance.

☐ Experiment with different effects – reverb, echo, distortion, etc. for different tracks.

Tips for Making a Good Recording

1. Work in a room where there is little to no natural echo.

2. Silence everything you don't want the microphone to record.

3. Use an external microphone and the best quality that you can access.

4. Work close to the microphone.

5. Block wind (air from heating systems, fans, etc.) from reaching your microphone.

6. Check your levels before you record. A range of -6 to -12 decibels is best. This may initially sound quiet to you, but it will allow you increase the volume without distortion.

7. If you will need to align different tracks, use a metronome and make a sound 4 beats before you begin playing. This sound can be used make different tracks line up.

Source: Created by Michele Kaschub and Janice P. Smith with images from iStock/Credit: tostphoto.

Chapter 17

Spoken Word and Music

Intermediate Level

Composition Strand: Music Theater

About this Project

Works of music theater often present complex stories featuring multiple viewpoints woven together in dialogue and song. These works are often large in scale and expensive to produce, but smaller scale works can have similar artistic impact.

Spoken Word Poetry (SWP) and music composition can be partnered to allow students opportunities to artistically explore important ideas. SWP is a branch of creative writing in which poets express their point of view (POV) through the writing and performance of free verse. When partnered with music composition, SWP can serve to enhance and expand students' critical-thinking skills as they analyze and consider the multifaceted nature of an issue that they find relevant to their lives. The process of packaging these understandings in an artistic form empowers students to discover their self-identities and creative voices through the acts of creative writing, composing, and performing.

In this project, students will practice artistic democratic engagement with issues of social justice by selecting a topic and message that they wish to explore and present to their peers. Students will exercise their artistic autonomy as they engage in the processes of selecting and crafting poetic and musical materials into expressive products, explore the multidimensionality of artistic forms, and collaborate with peers to produce and share a product representing their unique viewpoints.

National Arts Standards for Music

This lesson presents students with an opportunity to:

- MU:Cr1.1.8a. Generate rhythmic, melodic, and harmonic phrases and harmonic accompaniments within expanded forms (including introductions, transitions, and codas) that convey expressive intent
- MU:Cr2.1.8a. Select, organize, and document personal musical ideas for arrangements, songs, and compositions within expanded forms that demonstrate tension and release, unity and variety, balance, and convey expressive intent.
- MU:Cr3.1.8a. Evaluate their own work by selecting and applying criteria including appropriate application of compositional techniques, style, form, and use of sound sources.
- MU:Cr3.1.8b. Describe the rationale for refining works by explaining the choices, based on evaluation criteria.
- MU:Cr3.2.8a. Present the final version of their documented personal composition, song, or arrangement, using craftsmanship and originality to demonstrate the application of compositional techniques for creating unity and variety, tension and release, and balance to convey expressive intent.
- MU:Re7.2.6a. Describe how the elements of music and expressive qualities relate to the structure of the pieces.
- MU:Re8.1.6a. Describe a personal interpretation of how creators' and performers' application of the elements of music and expressive qualities, within genres and cultural and historical context, convey expressive intent.

- MU:Re9.1.8a. Apply appropriate personally developed criteria to evaluate musical works or performances.
- MU:Cn10.0.7a. Demonstrate how interests, knowledge, and skills relate to personal choices and intent when creating, performing, and responding to music.
- MU:Cn11.0.7a. Demonstrate understanding of relationships between music and the other arts, other disciplines, varied contexts, and daily life.

Materials

- A set of project *Sketchpages*
- Software or apps for creating and editing music (Audacity, Garageband, Musescore), and videos (iMovie, MovieMaker); RemixLive and Figure
- Copies of the *Guidelines for Preparing for Performance*
- A *Critical Reflection Guide* for each composer (see appendix B)

Project Time

- This project will take four to five class periods. Class time can be abbreviated if students complete writing and rehearsals as homework.

DISCUSSION QUESTIONS TO DEVELOP COMPOSITIONAL CAPACITIES

? Feelingful Intention—What feeling do you hope that the audience will associate with your message?
? Musical Expressivity—While any of the MUSTS may play a crucial role in shaping how the audience receives this work, unity-variety and tension-release are often highly influential in the performance of SWP. Which of the devices appearing in the poetry have you chosen to parallel in the music? Why?
? Artistic Craftsmanship—The partnership between the poem and the music can be expressed through complimentary writing, contrasted writing, or even through the creation of an ambient soundscape that is not specifically timed to poetic events. Which compositional path did you decide to pursue and why?

SEQUENCE OF ACTIVITIES

Phase 1—Exploring SWP

- Ask the students what they know about SWP and poetry slams. If students are unfamiliar with this genre, find a few online videos to watch and discuss.
- Invite the students to talk about the poems they have heard. What topics were featured? Why do they think the performer chose to address these topics?
- Ask the students to describe how SWP is performed. What are the typical performance settings? How do the performers present themselves and their poems?
- Have the students brainstorm ideas about how music might be used to enhance the presentation of SWP. (MU:Cn11.0.7a)
- Discuss with the students how they would like to proceed with creating a SWP and music performance. Students might like to work individually to create an original poem with music or they may prefer to work in pairs with one student taking lead on poetry and the other on music. Both working conditions will expose students to similar processes, but project work times may vary as co-creators will need time to collaborate in class.

Phase 2—Think and Write

- Distribute the *Creating SWP Sketchpage* and discuss subject selection, POV, convictions, and having the courage to present your own views.

- Give students some class time to get started. They may need to do some research to learn more about their chosen topic. This phase may be completed in class or assigned as homework.
- Meet with individual students or collaborative teams to discuss their initial ideas and answer any questions they may have about creating their poems.
- Work with students to set deadlines for completing the first draft and final version of the poem.

Phase 3—Consider the Poem-Music Partnership

- Now that students have their poems in hand, take time to discuss the specific role of music when partnered with SWP. Students should come to understand that the musical component of this partnership is intended to envelope the audience in an emotional state while they deliver their message. In this partnership, the music can assume a form which complements or contrasts the text, or which may have an ambient quality that defines a time, space, or general mood.
- Distribute the *Partnering Poetry and Music Sketchpage*. Guide students through the first few steps of analyzing their poem to identify musical potentials. (MU:Re7.2.6a) Invite students to share a few text lines and musical ideas with the class for feedback and discussion before encouraging students to complete their analysis on their own. (MU:Cr2.1.8a)
- Once students have a few initial ideas, encourage them to take out instruments, computers, or smart devices to begin crafting their music. Students may find it helpful to record their SWP on one track. They can then add loops or record additional tracks to complete their musical accompaniment. (MU:Cr1.1.8a)

Phase 4—Prepare for Performance

- Most students will have given some sort of verbal presentation to a class by the time they are in middle school, but few will have been called upon to give an impassioned performance representing an idea that is important to them.
- Take time to discuss with students the difference between purposeful performance (the intentional delivery of an artistic idea) and expression (an emotional outlet).
- Distribute the *Guidelines for Preparing for Performance*. Discuss each of the rehearsal ideas with the students and address any questions they may have.
- Allow time for at-home practice so that students can feel prepared to share their performances with their classmates.

Phase 5—Sharing and Discussion

- Create a time for each poet or poet/composer team to present their work. (MU:Cr3.2.8a)
- Take time to ask the creators about how they partnered text and music to create the feelingful intention that they sought. (MU:Cr3.1.8a; MU:Cr3.1.8b)
- Ask the audience to identify poetic and musical devices used to create an impactful artwork. (MU:Re8.1.6a)

Phase 6—Reflection and Self-Assessment

- Distribute copies of the *Critical Reflections Guide* and have each student reflect on what they learned as they worked through this project. (MU:Cr3.1.8a; MU:Cr3.1.8b; MU:Re9.1.8a; MU:Cn10.0.7a)

Optional Extension

1. Partner with ELA class to have the language arts students create poems and the music students create the musical partners.
2. Partner with social studies class studying a historical period or event. Create a poetry and music partnership representative of the time in both artistic style and substance to offer a period performance imbued with modern sensibilities.

Source: Created by Michele Kaschub and Janice P. Smith with images from iStock/Credit: twinsterphoto.

Partnering Poetry & Music

Copy your poem here and then mark it with your analysis.

Top arrows (pointing down):

- Describe a few musical sounds might offer a similar affect.
- List sounds that could be repeated to create unity or added to create variety.
- How might you create musical "space" for sound evoking words to be heard?
- What compositional devices might be used to heighten tension or facilitate its release?
- How can the music be shaped to enhance how the audience experiences these turns?

Bottom arrows (pointing up):

- Where does the poem need to move forward? Hang back? Draw forward and backward arrows over the text.
- Are there devices that create unity in the poem? Circle these and draw lines to connect them. Star ideas that offer variety.
- Are there any words that have special sounds (i.e., slam, bang, whisper)? Draw a box around these.
- How is the balance of tension and release presented in this work? Double underline points of tension.
- Is the poem stable or are there unexpected events? Draw explosion circles around de-stablilizers.

Source: Created by Michele Kaschub and Janice P. Smith.

Guidelines for Preparing Your Performance

- ☐ Practice, practice, practice! Spoken word poems are meant to be performed. Try saying each line a few different ways and determine which delivery has the greatest impact.

- ☐ In music, a score is the blueprint for musical sounds. Take a clean copy of your poem and use it as a study score. Mark quiet or subtle lines in blue, hot and fiery lines in red, things that need to be said quickly with green forward arrows. Place an apostrophe or checkmark where you plan to breathe – and make the breath meaningful.

- ☐ Eye contact is critical for connecting with the audience. Draw eyes on the study score in places where you want to lock eyes with the audience or an eye with an arrow for "scan eyes across audience". These stage directions will help you convey your ideas to the audience as you perform.

- ☐ Project your voice. Your poem can only have an impact if the audience can hear it. Consider the use of dynamics. Where will you speak more quietly or more loudly? Mark these with a "p" (piano/quiet) or "f" (forte/loud).

- ☐ Enunciate. Similar to projection, speaking clearly will help the audience understand what you are saying. Works can be delivered with different types of articulation. Are there words that you will say very evenly? Words that you will speak sharply or with additional emphasis? Consonants like "t" or "p" that you want to have bite? Highlight these.

- ☐ Move to a mirror. What does your face say while you are delivering your poem? Is your facial expression reflective of the mood you hope to convey? Make faces in the mirror until you find the ones that best fit the feeling behind your words. This will feel a little weird at first, but actors do it all the time.

- ☐ Use gestures. Simple hand movements, taking a step towards or away from the audience, nodding your head, extending your arms, or bouncing up and down, can all add emphasis and increase the emotional impact in your performance.

- ☐ Engage your memory. In this project you will have two components to time, your recitation of the poem and the recorded (or live performance) music. Practice these elements until they become so routine that they feel naturally intertwined. This level of familiarity with your work will allow you to more fully engage with your audience.

- ☐ Hold a dress rehearsal. You don't have to dress up but perform the work for someone who will give you constructive feedback. Listen to the suggestions they offer, evaluate their ideas, practice some more, and repeat until you feel ready to perform.

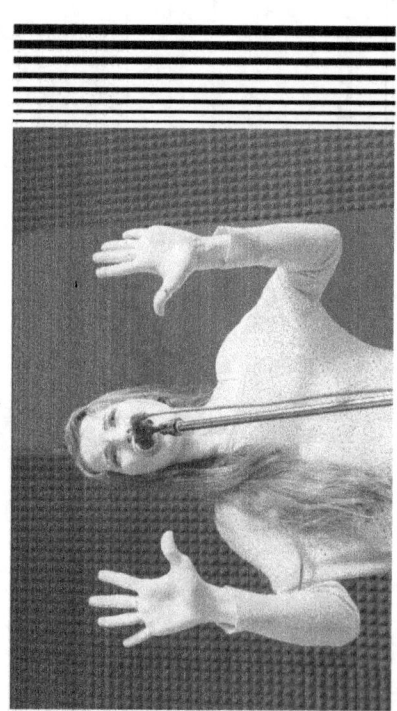

Source: Created by Michele Kaschub and Janice P. Smith with images from iStock/Credit: golubovy.

# PROJECTS FOR ADVANCED COMPOSERS

Chapter 18

Creating a Jazz Vocal

Advanced Level

Composition Strand: Songwriting

About this Project

Musical tasks such as composing for big band or performing virtuosic jazz improvisations often begin with the creation of a simply notated sketch called a lead sheet. Jazz musicians, in particular, use lead sheets to capture the key musical ideas featured in their performances. They then discuss how they will interpret those ideas, often using common backing patterns, to perform the music.

To develop an understanding of how musicians might organize their musical thinking, students will form groups and work together to compose an original jazz tune. Students will listen to exemplar charts to identify stylistic characteristics of jazz. Their observations will be matched with an introduction to entry-level jazz harmony before they begin to create their original jazz vocal which they will preserve in lead sheet form.

National Arts Standards for Music

This lesson presents students with an opportunity to:

- MU:Cr2.1.8b. Use standard and/or iconic notation and/or audio/video recording to document personal rhythmic phrases, melodic phrases, and harmonic sequences.
- MU:Cr3.1.8a. Evaluate their own work by selecting and applying criteria including appropriate application of compositional techniques, style, form, and use of sound sources.
- MU:Cr3.1.8b. Describe the rationale for refining works by explaining the choices, based on evaluation criteria.
- MU:Re7.2.6a. Describe how the elements of music and expressive qualities relate to the structure of the pieces.
- MU:Re7.2.6b. Identify the context of music from a variety of genres, cultures, and historical periods.
- MU:Re8.1.6a. Describe a personal interpretation of how creators' and performers' application of the elements of music and expressive qualities, within genres and cultural and historical context, convey expressive intent.
- MU:Re8.1.7a. Describe a personal interpretation of contrasting works and explain how creators' and performers' application of the elements of music and expressive qualities, within genres, cultures, and historical periods, convey expressive intent.
- MU:Re9.1.8a. Apply appropriate personally developed criteria to evaluate musical works or performances.
- MU:Cn10.0.8a. Demonstrate understanding of relationships between music and the other arts, other disciplines, varied contexts, and daily life.

Materials

- A *What do I hear?* listening guide for each student
- A *Creating A Jazz Vocal Lead Sheet Sketchpage* packet for each composer

- Audio/video examples of several jazz charts featuring vocalists
- Access to drum set, guitar, bass guitar, piano, microphone and small amp for vocalist; or app/software equivalents
- A *Critical Reflection Guide* for each composer (see appendix B)

Project Time

- It will take approximately four to six class periods to listen and introduce technical foundations; compose and notate the chart; prepare the chart for performance; and perform and receive feedback from peers.

DISCUSSION QUESTIONS TO DEVELOP COMPOSITIONAL CAPACITIES

? Feelingful Intention—What feeling or feelings will be explored through this chart?
? Musical Expressivity—Which of the MUSTS is most influential within this chart? Why?
? Artistic Craftsmanship—How might lyrics and melody be partnered to invite performers and listeners to engage with the feeling aspect of this chart? In what way does the harmonic language of jazz influence what is expressed in this tune?

SEQUENCE OF ACTIVITIES

Phase 1—Creating a Shared Background

- Distribute a copy of the *What do I hear?* listening guide to each student. Invite students to critically analyze a few recordings of jazz vocalists such as Ella Fitzgerald, Diana Krall, Nancy Wilson, Esperanza Spalding, Jazzmeia Horn, Louis Armstrong, Tony Bennett, Jacob Collier, Elliot Skinner, or others. Help students to identify the key features of each song. If possible, listen to a few selections arranged for combo and big band. Discuss the differences between these arrangements. For example, *Slap That Bass* by George and Ira Gershwin is an example of a widely recorded jazz tune that can be heard in big band, combo, and choral arrangements. (MU:Re7.2.6b)
- Have students make a list of the musical ideas or features that they hear as you guide them to consider:
  ○ What instruments do you hear?
  ○ What is the role of each instrument?
  ○ How does the voice function in the arrangement (delivers melody, scats like an instrument, or something else)?
  ○ How is each song organized?
  ○ What musical gestures do you hear from the instruments? For example, does the bass play a single repeating note, play the notes of the chord in succession, or "walk" the line by occasionally inserting notes between those of the chord.
  ○ Does the tune sound like other music that you listen to or is it different in some way? Guide students to consider the swing rhythms, harmonies, and instrumentation, if possible. (MU:Re7.2.6a)
- Conclude this aural investigation by having students create a list of the features they think are absolutely critical in making music "sound jazzy." (MU:Re8.1.7a)

Phase 2—Introducing Lead Sheets

- Project or distribute copies of a lead sheet to students. First, ask students to identify the notation, symbols, and other items that they recognize. Then, encourage students to identify notational elements that are new to them. Take time to decipher each of these notational symbols. Items that might be identified include:
  ○ Clef, key signature, time signature
  ○ Tempo and style indicators

- Chord symbols. Note that chord symbols represent an "harmonic region" and stay in effect until the next chord symbol appears.
- Discuss how to decode a chord symbol. The letter name represents the root of the chord. The triad quality is represented with letters or symbols. The list below is meant to be a reminder for those who may not use this musical language on a regular basis. This chord collection is far more extensive than what students will need to know for this lesson.
    - major: Maj or M—as DMaj7 or DM7
    - minor: min or—as Dmin or D-
    - dominant seventh chord as D7
    - half-diminished as Dmin7♭5 or D-7♭5
    - diminished: dim or ° as Ddim or D°
    - augmented: aug or + as Daug or D+
    - extended tones such as 9, 11, or 13 as D7(11)
    - alterations (non-diatonic tones) D7(9)
    - bass note other than chord root as D7/A
- The melodic line may or may not include dynamic indications or articulations as these are often left to the singer to determine
- Roadmap indicators: repeat signs, multiple endings, codas, del segnos, etc
- Lyrics

Phase 3—Composing the Tune/Creating the Lead Sheet

- Have students form groups of 3–5
- Each group needs at least one instrument or device and app that can produce chords.
- Distribute a copy of the *Jazz Vocal Lead Sheet Sketchpage* to each group. Provide an overview of the sheets, as needed. (MU:Cr2.1.8b)
- Establish a working goal for the class period: "By [time] your group should complete [indicate task from *Sketchpage*]." This helps students learn to divide their project into small, achievable steps.
- Review instructions for the sections to be completed, set students to work, and then circulate through the classroom and be available to assist groups as needed.

Phase 4—Analysis and Sharing

- These works will be presented to the class. Encourage students to read through and discuss within their team the prompt questions on the final page of the *Sketchpage* packet. (MU:Cr3.1.8a)
- As the students share their work with the class, draw on this list of questions to invite critical reflection on what has been learned about jazz style, what has been experienced in the creation of the jazz vocal chart, and how students grasp the connections between the tools of artistic craftsmanship, the musical expressivities present in their pieces, and the feelingful intentions that underlie their work. (MU:Re8.1.6a)

Phase 5—Reflection and Self-Assessment

- The *Critical Reflections Guide* located in the appendix can serve as a useful tool for fostering the skills of reflection and self-assessment. (MU:Cr3.1.8a; MU:Cr3.1.8b; MU:Re9.1.8a; MU:Cn10.0.8a)

Optional Extension

Following performance, these lead sheets can be used to further skills in arranging and improvisation.

- To continue in a compositional focus, lead sheets can be expanded upon to create arrangements for combos or big band.
- Lead sheets can be useful tools for improvisation as students can discuss the various ways the melodic content and harmonic ideas can be presented in new and different ways.

WHAT DO I HEAR?

Song: **Singer:**

- What instruments do I hear?
- What is the role of each instrument?
- What does the voice do in this arrangement?
- How is the piece organized?
- What musical ideas do I hear?
- How does this tune sound the same or different than others I have heard?
- Other things I heard:

Song: **Singer:**

- What instruments do I hear?
- What is the role of each instrument?
- What does the voice do in this arrangement?
- How is the piece organized?
- What musical ideas do I hear?
- How does this tune sound the same or different than others I have heard?
- Other things I heard:

Song: **Singer:**

- What instruments do I hear?
- What is the role of each instrument?
- What does the voice do in this arrangement?
- How is the piece organized?
- What musical ideas do I hear?
- How does this tune sound the same or different than others I have heard?
- Other things I heard:

Song: **Singer:**

- What instruments do I hear?
- What is the role of each instrument?
- What does the voice do in this arrangement?
- How is the piece organized?
- What musical ideas do I hear?
- How does this tune sound the same or different than others I have heard?
- Other things I heard:

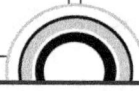

Source: Created by Michele Kaschub and Janice P. Smith with images from iStock/Credit: Elena Shikova.

CREATING A JAZZ VOCAL LEAD SHEET

Choose A Simple Jazz Chord Progression

The 2-5-1 chord progression is one of the most common building blocks of jazz songs. In this lesson the progression will be used in a major key. The chord changes are often written as ii-V-I to show the major and minor quality of the chords. In the key of D major, this progression might be written as Em7, A7, DMaj7. Simply notated, the ii-V-I progression might look like this:

The progression notated for piano and guitar (in tablature) might appear as shown below. Notice that the notes of each chord have been spread out across the left and right hands for the piano. The root of the chord (the note the chord is named for) is the lowest pitch as each chord is shown below. Putting the root note in the bass (lowest position) can give harmonic strength to the chord. Take a few minutes to play this chord progression on the guitar or piano or enter it into a notation software program so that you can hear the harmonic movement of the changing chords.

While whole songs have and can be written using just three chords, jazz musicians sometimes replace one chord with another to change the emotive quality of progression. One common change is to use a 6 (vi) chord instead of the I chord. Because the DMaj7 (D, F#, A, C#) and the Bm7 (B, D, F# A) share three pitches, the substitution sounds right to the ear. Notice, though, the chord quality changes from major (I) to minor (vi). Take a few minutes to explore this substitution. You could replace both DMaj7 chords with Bm7. You could also use them in either order (DMaj7-Bm7 or Bm7-DMaj7).

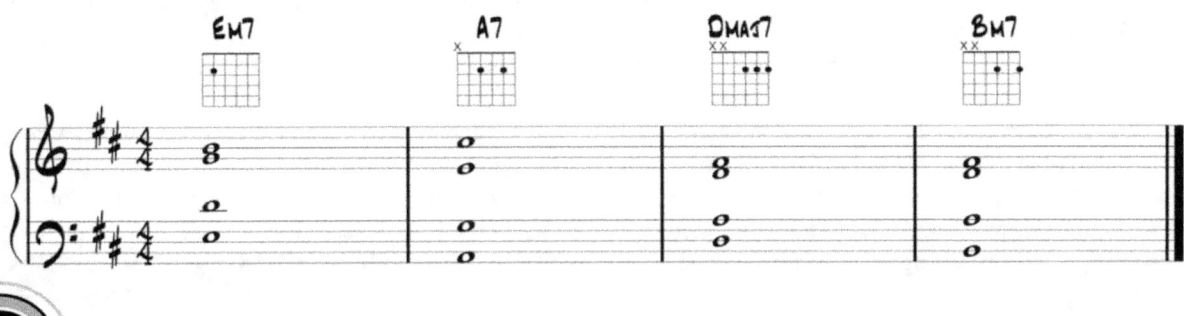

Source: Created by Michele Kaschub and Janice P. Smith.

Build Your Lead Sheet

Notate your chord progression on the lead sheet below. If you are notating for piano and wish to fully notate the pitches for each chord, request a larger sheet of staff paper from your teacher. You may write chord names (DMaj7, Em7, A7 or Bm7) where you wish. You might decide to play one chord per measure or multiple chords as fits the needs of your song.

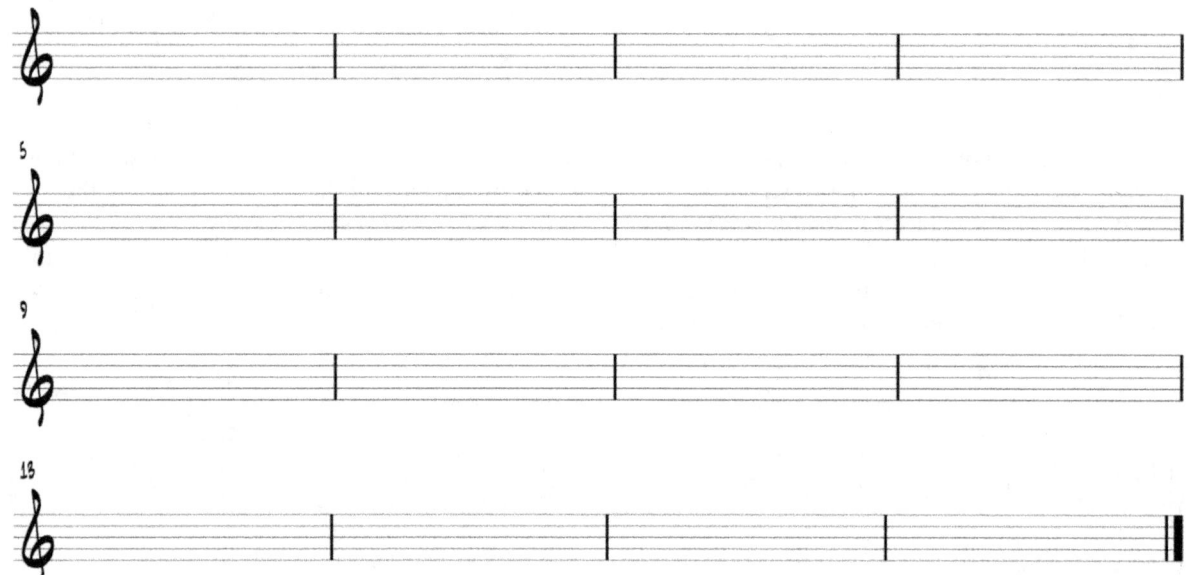

Writing the Vocal

There are several different ways to write a vocal. As this chart (jazz song) uses just 3 or 4 chords, it is easiest to begin with harmony and add a melody and lyrics. Play the chord progression several times. If possible, record the progression and let it play as a loop.

Hum or sing on "doo or loo" over your chord progression. Remember how the jazz vocalists used their voices to emphasize or shape certain sounds and words? Experiment. Don't rush. It may take a little time to find just the right melody. When you think you've got it, maybe even just one line, record it. It is easy to lose track of a good tune while you work on finding the rest of it!

Some songwriters like to figure out the entire melody of a song before they add lyrics, others write lyrics first and then craft a melody to fit both words and chord progressions at the same time. You may find that a mix of these approaches works. If you think of words as you hum or sing over the chord progression, write them down. Once you've got your lyrics, write them on the lead sheet above being sure to match words with chord changes. After this is done, you can notate your melody.

Source: Created by Michele Kaschub and Janice P. Smith.

Prepare to Share

Practice singing and playing your jazz vocal until your team feels ready to share it with the class. You might decide that everyone sings, that two people sing, or that one member of your team is ready to solo. If using acoustic instruments, other members of the group should remember to play a little quieter than the singer(s) so that the lyrics can be heard.

Here are some things you might think about before your team shares its composition. Make notes about what you'd like to say and who on your team is going to say it.

1. How will you introduce your jazz chart?

2. Does it have a title?

3. Where did the title come from?

4. Does it have a special, silly or other background story?

5. What parts of your piece best represent jazz style?

6. Is there anything in your jazz vocal that was influenced by one or more of the jazz vocalists you heard at the beginning of this project? Another singer?

7. Is there anything you would like your classmates to listen for as you share your composition?

8. Is there any part of your jazz chart that you are very proud of? What is it? Why are you proud of that work?

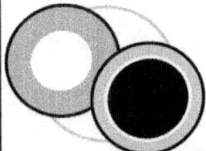

Source: Created by Michele Kaschub and Janice P. Smith.

Chapter 19

Scoring Dynamic Documentaries

Advanced Level

Composition Strand: Film Scoring

About this Project

Documentaries focus on current or historical events, social experiences, or natural phenomena. They educate the audience. They can spark discussion about real issues. This project places students in pairs to create a short documentary and compose a soundtrack to support its message. This is an advanced project that is best suited for students who have had some hands-on experience with filmmaking, movie editing software, and basic music recording and editing software. It may be helpful to students to complete the *Public Service Announcement* and *One Scene, Many Interpretations* projects before undertaking this one.

National Arts Standards for Music

This lesson presents students with an opportunity to:

- MU:Cr2.1.8a. Select, organize, and document personal musical ideas for arrangements, songs, and compositions within expanded forms that demonstrate tension and release, unity and variety, balance, and convey expressive intent.
- MU:Cr2.1.8b. Use standard and/or iconic notation and/or audio/ video recording to document personal rhythmic phrases, melodic phrases, and harmonic sequences.
- MU:Cr3.1.8a. Evaluate their own work by selecting and applying criteria including appropriate application of compositional techniques, style, form, and use of sound sources.
- MU:Cr3.1.8b. Describe the rationale for refining works by explaining the choices, based on evaluation criteria.
- MU:Cr3.2.8a. Present the final version of their documented personal composition, song, or arrangement, using craftsmanship and originality to demonstrate the application of compositional techniques for creating unity and variety, tension and release, and balance to convey expressive intent.
- MU:Re8.1.6a. Describe a personal interpretation of how creators' and performers' application of the elements of music and expressive qualities, within genres and cultural and historical context, convey expressive intent.
- MU:Re9.1.8a. Apply appropriate personally developed criteria to evaluate musical works or performances.
- MU:Cn10.0.8a. Demonstrate how interests, knowledge, and skills relate to personal choices and intent when creating, performing, and responding to music.
- MU:Cn11.0.8a. Demonstrate understanding of relationships between music and the other arts, other disciplines, varied contexts, and daily life.

Materials

- *Note:* Before introducing this project to students, create a partnership with a school librarian. The school library and its staff can be an invaluable resource for students as they conduct the background research which will support their documentary.

- A complete set of *Sketchpages* for each student
- A *Critical Reflection Guide* for each composer (see appendix B)
- Video cameras or smart devices for filming the documentary
- A tripod or other device for holding the video camera/smart device steady
- An external microphone can improve the quality of sound recording
- Movie production software with sound manipulation capabilities. Free software is available.
- Instruments, notation software, or sample and looping software.
- Additional resources which may be helpful
  - Vision Video School Online https://vision.wettintv.de/?page_id=126
    This is an excellent and concise guide to making a documentary for teachers and students. It provides guidance for finding success and avoiding common mistakes.
  - How to Film a Powerful Documentary: A Step-by-Step Guide https://www.sheffieldav.com/education/guide-filming-powerful-documentary
    Designed for young adult or older filmmakers, this site provides a strong overview of key steps in the documentary-making process.

Project Time

- Eight to ten class meetings
- Additional time as homework for conducting research, interviews, and filming.
- Learning to manage deadlines is an important part of the process.

DISCUSSION QUESTIONS TO DEVELOP COMPOSITIONAL CAPACITIES

? Feelingful Intention—What is the overall tone of our documentary? How do we want the audience to feel as they watch and listen? Do we need a theme to connect the various parts or provide background for any of the material? What would the feeling of such a theme need to be? Will that feeling change at any point? To what?

? Musical Expressivity—How can music be used to reinforce key points in the film? Where might the music need more motion? Which of the MUSTS will unify the music used in our film? What types of sounds will best convey the feelings in our film? Where are the moments of dramatic tension and what musically can heighten that?

? Artistic Craftsmanship—Does the documentary need a theme to connect the various parts or provide background for any of the material? Is there a particular style of music that is important to this documentary? Note: This might be important if using historical material or material highlights some unique aspect of a particular culture.

SEQUENCE OF ACTIVITIES

Phase 1—Introducing Documentaries

- Open a discussion about documentaries. What are they? What purpose do they serve? Who makes them? Why? (MU:Cn11.0.8a)
- Show a few short clips. If possible, show examples of narrative, argumentative, poetic, and descriptive documentaries. Each type serves a different function:
  - *Narrative*: The filmmaker uses a narrator or interviewees tell the story.
  - *Argumentative*: The filmmaker presents a hypothesis with the narrator or interviewees making for and against arguments.
  - *Poetic*: The filmmaker aims to evoke particular feelings rather than presenting facts or arguing specific points.
  - *Descriptive*: The filmmaker uses narrator or interviewees talk about, or describe, one subtopic at a time to create a big picture view of the subject.

- Work with students to make a list of the types of materials and techniques used in these clips. These may include how the narrator is featured, how interviews are conducted, how the interviewees are shown, use of text appearing over the film or between interviews, use of props, backgrounds, lighting, and so on.

Phase 2—Planning the Documentary

- Help students form working pairs (or trios, as needed).
- Distribute copies of the *Documentary Planning Sketchpage* and provide students with a quick overview. This sheet will help students identify a topic that will have meaning to a particular audience. They will also be guided to select one of the four documentary styles introduced above to use as an organizational concept for their film. Give students 5 minutes to brainstorm and make an initial decision about these aspects of their work. (MU:Cn10.0.8a)
- Invite each documentary team to briefly share their topic, audience, and message with the class. Keep this brief. Just a minute per team. If two or more groups have chosen the same topic, explore how they might adopt different focal points or help them decide if anyone wishes to pursue a different topic. Use of the same topic is certainly acceptable, but the class may learn more if each team pursues a different topic.
- Guide the students to think about the research phase of their work. Remind them that documentaries are nonfiction. What is the history behind their topic? What are the facts surrounding their topic? How do they know they have found facts and not opinions? How can they shed a positive light on their topic? What do they want audience members to do once they have gained a better understanding of the topic presented in the documentary?
- Draw attention to the second page of the *Documentary Planner Sketchpage* and encourage students to make lists and take notes about key resources, interviewees, and artifacts.

Phase 3—Plan a Trip to the Library/Computer Lab

- Students may be able to conduct basic web searches as part of their homework for this project. However, some students may have limited access to these types of resources outside of school. Teams may benefit from a trip to the school computer lab, school library, or even local library to access pictures, graphics, maps, archival material, or other resources unique to the focus of their documentaries. It also may be possible for students to do this work during study halls or in afterschool hours.

Phase 4—Creating a Synopsis, Storyboard, and the Video Recording Plan

- With initial planning completed, teachers may want to impose an overall time limit (length) on these projects to keep them manageable. Young filmmakers tend to want to include every thought they have had as they have planned their documentary. As they advance to creating the synopsis of their film, they can begin to make critical inclusion/exclusion decisions. Beginning this process now will allow them to make wise decisions that will facilitate more effective final edits.
- Encourage students to write a brief overview of their documentary using the *Synopsis and Storyboard Sketchpage* before completing the *Video Recording Plan*. These guides will help them organize their thinking. They will identify locations where they may wish to film, ideas they hope to emphasize about their focus topic, interviewees they hope to speak with, and what questions they hope to ask each person they have identified.
- Schedule recording times and obtain any necessary permissions.

Phase 5—Record Scenes

- Take time to discuss the basics of good videography.
  - Check the light. People's faces should be clear. Shots of locations should be bright (unless dark and scary is the goal). Imagine the filming area to be a triangle. One angle is the light, one is the camera, and the remaining one is the person or place being filmed.

- Keep backgrounds visually calm. Place interviewees in front of solid color walls or gentle repeating patterns like brick. Have the subject stand or sit 5–6 feet away from the wall to avoid casting a shadow on the background.
- Get clean and clear audio. Try to conduct interviews or narrations in a quiet location. Even if the point is that an area is "too noisy," the viewer still needs to hear the message.
- If filming on a phone, use the back camera. It is usually the better camera on the phone.
- Hold the video recording device still. Use a tripod, a stack of books, or anything that will keep the video from shaking.
- Use the rule of thirds. Imagine that a tic-tac-toe board is drawn on the camera view lens. The four spots where the lines intersect are visually the most interesting places to put the subject of the shot.
- Shoot from a variety of angles to add interest. When changing perspectives, go big. Little changes are too subtle.
- Encourage students to divide filming tasks. One person should do the videography and the other person should do the interviewing.
- Have students practice asking the interview questions of someone they are not going to interview for the documentary. This will help them determine if their questions are clear.
- Remind students to use external microphones, if they are available, as this will produce a better quality of sound.
- Instruct students to record as much video as possible, as they will not have time to return to offsite locations.
- Remind students that they may want to record sounds that are not interviews. For example, a documentary about efforts to clean up a park might benefit from audio clips of birds chirping or children playing. Alternatively, these elements are Foley art and free audio clips of common sounds such as these can be found on the Internet.
- Insist that students thank the people who have helped them or contributed interviews. This is a good time to offer a mini-lesson on writing thank-you notes.

Phase 6—Build and Edit the Film

- At this point, students should have gathered all the video and other artifacts they need to assemble their documentaries.
- Before students set to work, acknowledge that they have reached a big step: the final selection of what to include and exclude from their documentary. This is a process which can be time-consuming and frustrating. Tell students to remember the documentary length that you have set (2, 3, or 5 minutes) and encourage them to use only those materials that emphasize their point.
- Encourage teams to organize their materials following their storyboard plan. They should then upload all footage and still shots, if any are to be included, into their movie editing software.
- Remind students to SAVE often. It can be helpful to save the project in multiple files as Draft 1, Draft 2, Draft 3, and so on, rather than overwriting and keeping just the latest version as work unfolds. Doing this will allow students to easily backtrack if they need to do so.

Phase 7—Creating the Film Score

- Once students are satisfied with the movie they have assembled, they need to turn their attention to the creation of their film score. This is a good time for the class to revisit the documentary clips viewed at the outset of this project with an ear toward what kind of music film score composers have used at different points. As the clips play, invite students to consider:
  - What do introduction typically sound like?
  - Are there musical themes present in the documentary?
  - What kind of music is used at points of tension?
  - When the story releases tension and seeks to put a hopeful spin on resolving a troubling issue, what happens to the music? (MU:Re8.1.6a)
- Distribute a copy of the *Creating the Film Score Sketchpage* to each team. Review the key questions with the class and then be available to assist teams as students begin to create their scores. (MU:Cr2.1.8a)

- If students are using acoustic instruments, they will need a quiet space to record their performances. If students are working in fully digital environments with notation or looping or sequencing software, headphones are most helpful in allowing all teams to easily hear their work without the distraction of hearing other teams testing their ideas. (MU:Cr2.1.8b)
- Students will be eager to show work that they are particularly proud of to their peers. Encourage a little of this as peer feedback can be helpful. Too much of a good thing, though, can become a distraction that will slow the completion process. It may be good to establish a particular time for sharing. For example, you might say, "Today at 1:00 p.m., we will take 5 minutes for you to share a trouble spot or a triumph with another team. If you share trouble spot, you might ask the other team for ideas that may help you." (MU:Re9.1.8a)
- Be aware that movie editing and music production software varies. Students may be able to complete all work in one program or they may need to import sound files into film editing platforms. Make sure that you have reviewed the steps needed to do this. It is also helpful if you make a "quick guide" to share with students to help them in completing these steps.
- Once the music is paired with the film, remind students to record any voiceovers they may need and to check sound levels. It is important that the audience be able to hear spoken word over the film score.

Phase 8—Film Festival

- It is important that students have an opportunity to share their documentaries. While in-class sharing is certainly the easiest course of action, it will be additionally rewarding for students to reach a larger audience with their work. Consider holding a screening for the full-grade level or as a school assembly if appropriate given the nature of the documentaries. Another option might be to host an afterschool or evening screening that is open to families or the community-at-large. If none of these beyond the classroom showings can be arranged, consider posting student work to a class website where students can then show it to family and friends. (MU:Cn3.2.8a)

Phase 9—Reflection and Self-Assessment

- Once students have had an opportunity to share their work and view the work of others, facilitate a discussion about creating documentaries. Ask the students to identify what they found to be rewarding in the project? What did they think about how the audience reacted to their work? What, if anything, would they do differently if they were to make another documentary? Did they encounter any challenges as they worked? How did they address these challenges? What advice might they give to next year's class about making documentaries?
- Distribute copies of the *Critical Reflection Guide* to each student and have them reflect on their working processes and final product. (MU:Cr3.1.8a; MU:Cr3.1.8b; MU:Re9.1.8a; MU:Cn10.0.8a)

Optional Extensions

Intergenerational Studies: Organize the class to interview sentient, elderly people in their homes or nursing facilities around a particular topic. For example, students might ask seniors about the music they enjoyed throughout their lives, important historical events they lived through, how some aspect of living has changed during their lives, etc.

Our Town: In conjunction with a social studies class, students might explore the work of various public servants and their roles in the community.

Our School: Students might focus on a service issue (how sustainability and recycling work in relation to meal service), or what different professionals in a school do (resource officer, librarian, occupational therapist, speech therapist, guidance counselor, etc.), or address a resource topic (how to get help with . . .).

Reframe any project to be undertaken by the whole class rather than in pairs or teams. Whole-class projects can be longer and involve different people doing various tasks. For example, several teams of students might conduct intergenerational interviews for the project described above, but then all of the interviews would be assembled into a single documentary and scored by the whole class.

Documentary Planner

Identify your audience:

- ❏ Peers
- ❏ Parents
- ❏ Teachers
- ❏ School Administrators
- ❏ Public
- ❏ Other?

Select a **topic** that your audience will care about, but not necessarily agree on. Our topic is:

Choose a **structure**. Will the documentary be:

- ❏ **narrative:** narrator or interviewees tell the story;
- ❏ **argumentative:** presents an hypothesis with the narrator or interviewees making for and against arguments;
- ❏ **poetic:** aiming to evoke particular feelings rather than presenting facts or arguing specific points; or,
- ❏ **descriptive:** narrator or interviewees talk about, or describe, one subtopic at a time?

Do the **research**:

What is the **history** surrounding this topic?	What are the **facts** about this topic? How do we know?

How can we frame information about this issue in a **positive** light?	How will our audience **know what to do** once they are more informed?

Source: Created by Michele Kaschub and Janice P. Smith with images from iStock/Credit: fergregory.

Documentary Planner - page 2

Questions we need to answer about our topic:

People we hope to interview:

Materials we wish to show such as pictures, graphics, maps, animations, archival material, other print or video material.

Source: Created by Michele Kaschub and Janice P. Smith.

Synopsis

Write a brief summary of the major points of the documentary. State the main points that will be presented. Name any key figures who will be interviewed.

Storyboard

Write a short description of each scene of the documentary in the order that they will be shown.

Source: Created by Michele Kaschub and Janice P. Smith.

Scoring Dynamic Documentaries

Video Recording Plan	Appointment Date	Time	Location & Desired Shot	Narration or Interview Questions	If needed, permission to film granted by:	Thank-You Note Sent (√)

Source: Created by Michele Kaschub and Janice P. Smith.

Creating the Film Score

Creating music for a documentary presents unique compositional challenges. Consider these ideas as you begin to plan your film score:

- Documentaries are single products made of a collection of smaller moments that may be very different from one another. Smaller moments may mean lots of little compositions. How will unity and variety be balanced across the documentary?
- Documentaries seek to develop an idea over time. How can motion and stasis be used to advance the story being told?
- The critical points being made in a documentary may need some additional highlighting to really stick with the audience. How can tension and release be used to add extra emphasis to key points?
- Sound is a powerful tool in documentary building, but sometimes silence can provide an opportunity for the brain to process the message. A few moments of silence can have a big impact. Are there places where silence will be more powerful than sound?

Movie Music Timeline

Beginning: Making a First Impression

- Will a title sequence (music played at the introduction of the documentary) be used? If so, note on the timeline how long it will be and what the feelingful intention for the music is.
- Which of the M.U.S.T.S. is most important in creating the desired first impression?
- What tools or compositional techniques might be used to shape how the audience experiences the set-up of the documentary?
  ❑ Check this box when the title sequence music is composed.

Start Time/ End Time	Feelingful Intention	Music Expressivity (M.U.S.T.S.)	Artistic Craftsmanship (tools/techniques)

Ending: What Should the Audience Feel Now?

- Will music be played as the closing credits roll? If so, note these on the timeline with descriptions for each capacity.
- Note that this music may be the same as the music used for the title sequence, but if the feelingful intention needs to change to invite the audience to be more energized or reflective, then the music might need to be different.
  ❑ Check this box when the title sequence music is composed

Start Time/ End Time	Feelingful Intention	Music Expressivity (M.U.S.T.S.)	Artistic Craftsmanship (tools/techniques)

Source: Created by Michele Kaschub and Janice P. Smith.

Creating the Film Score – p. 2

Middle: The Journey through the Main Message of the Film
- Identify key moments in the film. Are there particular moments of dramatic tension that should be matched with tense music? If so, note these on the timeline with descriptions for each capacity.
- Are there places where the music needs to fall away or be very quiet in the background? Note these on the timeline?
- Will there be thematic music that helps draw key ideas together? If yes, what will that music sound like? Will it always be the same or will there be variations? Note on the timeline where original themes and variations will be used.
- Will voiceovers be used? If so, note times and consider sound levels. It is important that the audience be able to hear spoken word over the film score.

Movie Music Timeline

Start Time/ End Time	Feelingful Intention	Music Expressivity (MUSTS)	Artistic Craftsmanship (tools/techniques)

Ask for additional planning sheets, if needed.

Source: Created by Michele Kaschub and Janice P. Smith.

Chapter 20

Composing Idiomatic Solos

Advanced Level

Composition Strand: Instrumental Music

About this Project

In this lesson, students will compose music for a single unaccompanied instrument. This requires careful consideration of the instrument's capabilities and idiomatic functions as violating these traits often results in music that is unplayable by the performer. In preparation for composing, each student will develop an instrument profile based on careful analysis of recordings and information that they will gather from multiple data sources. Students then will conduct either a self-inventory of their performance skills (if they are to play their own compositions) or a performer interview to identify the specific skill set that will shape their work. Throughout the project, students will participate in Composers' Circles to engage in critical reflection on their compositional process and final musical products.

Compositions may take one of several forms:

- each student composes for their own instrument and performs their own work.
- each student composes for a friend's instrument and the friend performs the work.
- each student composes for an instrument where there is a more experienced (high school, college, or professional) instrumentalist to perform the work.

National Art Standards for Music

This lesson presents students with an opportunity to:

- MU:Cr2.1.8a. Select, organize, and document personal musical ideas for arrangements, songs, and compositions within expanded forms that demonstrate tension and release, unity and variety, balance, and convey expressive intent.
- MU:Cr2.1.8b. Use standard and/or iconic notation and/or audio/video recording to document personal rhythmic phrases, melodic phrases, and harmonic sequences.
- MU:Cr3.1.8a. Evaluate their own work by selecting and applying criteria including appropriate application of compositional techniques, style, form, and use of sound sources.
- MU:Cr3.1.8b. Describe the rationale for refining works by explaining the choices, based on evaluation criteria.
- MU:Cr3.2.8a. Present the final version of their documented personal composition, song, or arrangement, using craftsmanship and originality to demonstrate the application of compositional techniques for creating unity and variety, tension and release, and balance to convey expressive intent.
- MU:Re7.2.6a. Describe how the elements of music and expressive qualities relate to the structure of the pieces.

- MU:Re8.1.6a. Describe a personal interpretation of how creators' and performers' application of the elements of music and expressive qualities, within genres and cultural and historical context, convey expressive intent.
- MU:Re9.1.8a. Apply appropriate personally developed criteria to evaluate musical works or performances.
- MU:Cn10.0.8a. Demonstrate how interests, knowledge, and skills relate to personal choices and intent when creating, performing, and responding to music.

Materials

- A set of project *Sketchpages* for each composer
- Access to staff paper or notation software, Internet search capabilities or music reference books about instruments and orchestration
- A *Critical Reflection Guide* for each composer (see appendix B)

Project Time

- This project will include four phases: introduction/research; self-inventory of performance skill or performer interview; composition time/progress checks; and performance and reflection.
- Some components of this project may be completed outside of class.

DISCUSSION QUESTIONS TO DEVELOP COMPOSITIONAL CAPACITIES

? Feelingful Intention—What feelingful intentions are best suited for the focus instrument? What are the emotive qualities most commonly associated with the focus instrument? What other feelingful qualities can this instrument invite? Are there any qualities that seem outside of the instrument's technical or expressive capabilities?

? Musical Expressivity—Which of the MUSTS will be most prominently featured in the composition? Are there particular MUSTS that best suit the capabilities of this instrument? For example, flutes and clarinets often exhibit rhythmic motion with quick scale passages while similar passages are less common in lower pitched instruments such as trombone or tuba.

? Artistic Craftsmanship—What elemental components will be used to create an expressive balance in the featured MUSTS so that listeners will be able to connect with the composition?

SEQUENCE OF ACTIVITIES

Phase 1—Introduction and Research

- Open the lesson by inviting students to name all of the instruments that they know. Write this list where everyone can view it.
- Ask the students if they know of any composers who have created unaccompanied works for any instrument in the list. A few answers may emerge, but it is more likely that this literature will be a new area for students.
- Select a few familiar instruments to use for listening analysis. Possible examples include:
    a. Cello—Cello Suite No. 1 Gigue, J.S. Bach, https://www.youtube.com/watch?v=OLYIRx9n9ko
    b. Flute—Acra Sacra, Cynthia Folio, https://www.youtube.com/watch?v=F7Df7937b0g
    c. Clarinet—Sonatina para clarinete solo, Miklós Rózsa, https://www.youtube.com/watch?v=TPg7axRj5-Y
    d. Saxophone—Introduction, Dance and Furioso, Herbert Couf, https://www.youtube.com/watch?v=OWFOhOlzyBY
    e. Trumpet—Fantasy for Trumpet, Malcom Arnold, https://www.youtube.com/watch?v=s3b_iHqUue8
    f. Tuba—Suite for Unaccompanied Tuba: IV, Galop: Presto, David Zerkel, https://www.youtube.com/watch?v=Y4ykEQ4wrWo

- Before playing the first example for students, ask them to predict what they think they will hear as they listen to the [insert name of instrument]. Listen together and then ask students to identify what sounds matched their expectations and what sounds were unexpected. Repeat with a few more listening examples. Then ask, "How do you think you developed your ideas about what the [instrument] 'should' sound like?" (MU:Cn11.0.8a)
- Work the term "idiomatic" into the discussion. When used in relation to an instrument, idiomatic refers to the sounds most commonly attributed to that instrument. The challenge of crafting music that is idiomatic of an instrument is that the definition is always expanding. As new sounds and techniques are invented and used repeatedly by composers and performers, the idiom grows.
- Extend the conversation to identify the compositional problem of this project: Exactly how do composers know what to compose for specific instruments?
- Outline the composition project and specify which approach the students will be using:
  - each student composes for their own instrument and performs their own work.
  - each student composes for a friend's instrument and the friend performs the work.
  - each student composes for an instrument where there is a more experienced (high school, collegiate, or professional) instrumentalist to perform the work.
- Distribute the *Instrument Profile* for students to complete as they research their chosen instrument. Students might begin with YouTube videos (https://www.youtube.com/playlist?list=PLqR22EoucCyccs5J639SCefaM7mD9dMSz) from the Philharmonia Orchestra of London featuring performers introducing violin, viola, cello, double bass, flute, clarinet, oboe, *cor anglais*, bass clarinet, Eb clarinet, bassoon, contrabassoon, French horn, trumpet, trombone, bass trombone, tuba, timpani, percussion, harp, and celeste. (MU:Re7.1.6a)
- Once students have completed the profile of their selected instrument, create opportunities for students to share their findings with a peer. Students who are focusing on the same instrument are logical partners for comparing notes. If students have used different sources of information, discrepancies may arise and they may need to do a little more research. Sharing is also useful for students who have profiled different instruments. As these students listen to each other, they may be able to identify additional questions about the instrument that the researcher may wish to address before beginning their composition work.

Phase 2—Getting to Know the Performer

Now that students have become more familiar with their chosen instrument, it is time to consider the skill level of their intended performer. All composers want their compositions to be successfully performed. Taking time to learn about the skills of the person who will premiere the work is, therefore, an important step in preparing to compose.

- Distribute the *Performer Interview* guide and review the questions with the class.
- If students are also acting as the performers of their own work, they should use the guide to conduct a self-inventory of their own performance skills.
- If students are working with classmates as the performers of their work, they should take 10 minutes or so to conduct their interviews. Multiple interview sessions may be needed so that each composer-performer pair has sufficient time to converse.
- If composers are creating works for performers who are not part of the class, it may be possible to bring performers into the class to talk about their instrument/skills. It may also be possible to conduct interviews remotely, via email or other means, outside of class time.

Phase 3—Composition Time and Progress Checks

At this point, composers have gathered the information they need to begin to craft their compositions. This is a good time to review the compositional capacities of feelingful intention, musical expressivity, and artistic craftsmanship using the guiding questions presented under "Discussion Questions to Develop Compositional Capacities."

- Distribute the *Composition Planner* and *Musical Thoughts Sketchpages*. Review the product guidelines. Note that while exact product specifications are best left to the composer, a 32-bar composition in common time performed at 72 bpm will be just under 2 minutes in length.
- Encourage students to begin drafting their initial ideas. These ideas may be descriptive or musical notations. (MU:Cr2.1.8a; MU:Cr2.1.8b)
- Discuss how composition work will proceed. This project may be completed in class or as homework. If structured as a homework project, students may need time to check in with their performer during class. They also benefit from the feedback they receive when they share their drafts in Composer Circles as described on pp. 40–41 (MU:Re8.1.6a)
- The specific amount of time needed for students to complete this project may vary. If students undertake this project as homework, they will likely need a week to compose. Students will need another week for performers to prepare their works. Performances, with introduction and discussion, typically take about 5 minutes per composer.

Phase 4—Performance

- Performances of student compositions may occur in class or be offered in a public recital. In both cases, it is important that composers have an opportunity to meet with their performers, hear their work, and rehearse to refine their finished products. If a public performance is to be offered, students will need to practice the presentation of their composer comments and their performances in a dress rehearsal. (MU:Cr3.2.8a)

Phase 5—Reflection and Self-Assessment

- Following the performance, engage students in thinking critically about their learning, their compositional processes, and their musical products. This may be accomplished through class discussion or students may work independently.
- Distribute copies of the *Critical Reflection Guide* found in the appendix and invite students to consider their work. (MU:Cr3.1.8a; MU:Cr3.1.8b; MU:Re9.1.8a; MU:Cn10.0.8a)

Optional Extension

This project can be repeated with students composing for duos, trios, or quartets. Composers could work individually or collaboratively. Compositions might feature instruments with similar idiomatic functions (brass quintet) or instruments with contrasting functions (flute and tuba duet). The research and self-inventory/interview components of the project would be expanded to include multiple instruments and performers, but the remainder of the project would closely follow the suggested sequence of activities for solo compositions.

Instrument Profile

The featured instrument is:

_____

Listen to 3-5 recordings that feature the instrument that you have chosen.
Note what you hear on the table below.
These may be sounds that you will want to use in your composition.

Draw the appropriate clef for the instrument.
Notate the range and tessitura of the instrument.
Reminder: The range includes all the pitches the instrument can produce while tessitura refers to pitches that are most comfortable to play.

How might you describe the character, feeling or moods that this instrument invites? Can it invite others? ---	Describe the melodies played by this instrument. Are they stepwise, skippy, or full of leaps? What articulations do you hear? ---	What unique technical abilities does this instrument have? ---

Source: Created by Michele Kaschub and Janice P. Smith.

Performer Interview

Interview Questions:

1. How high and low can you play?

2. What is your comfortable playing range?

3. Are there any notes that are particularly difficult for you to play?

4. What keys are best for you?

5. How fast or slow can you play and while still maintaining a good sound?

6. What are the best sounds you can make on your instrument?

7. Are there any really cool or unexpected sounds that you can make?

8. What is really difficult to do on your instrument? Should I avoid using that in my composition?

9. Are there sounds I should avoid?

10. (For wind players) How often do you need breathe?

11. What articulations can you play?

12. Are there other things that I should know about your instrument?

13. Are there things I should keep in mind about your playing as I compose?

14. Other questions:

Source: Created by Michele Kaschub and Janice P. Smith.

Composition Planner

PROJECT GUIDELINES

- My composition must reflect some of the capabilities and idiomatic functions of the instrument as identified in my research.
- My composition must reflect the performer's technical and artistic capacities as identified through the self-inventory/performer interview.
- My composition must be of sufficient length to explore the instrument's potentials. Approximate time _____.

Feelingful Intention

What feelingful intentions are best suited for the focus instrument? What are the emotive qualities most commonly associated with the focus instrument? What other feelingful qualities can this instrument invite? Are there any qualities that seem outside of the instrument's technical or expressive capabilities?

Musical Expressivity

Which of the M.U.S.T.S. will be most prominently featured in the composition? Are there particular M.U.S.T.S. that best suit the capabilities of this instrument?

Artistic Craftsmanship

What elemental components will be used to create an expressive balance in the featured M.U.S.T.S. so that listeners will be able to connect with the composition?

Source: Created by Michele Kaschub and Janice P. Smith.

148 Chapter 20

Musical Thoughts

Pro tip: Computers can produce music that humans and instruments will not be able to play. Make sure that your music is made for humans.

Pro Tip: Minimize the amount of time the performer spends playing at the outer edges their range and maximize time spent within their more comfortable tessitura.

Pro tip: Consider the skill level of the performer. Pieces that are too difficult for the performer to play with accuracy and artistry will be disappointing to you as you will not hear what you have imagined.

Source: Created by Michele Kaschub and Janice P. Smith.

Chapter 21

Environmental Musics

Advanced Level

Composition Strand: Electronic Music and Digital Media

About this Project

Ecological sounds, the focus of this project, are sounds found within environments. People who study ecoacoustics describe environmental sounds as the audible product of the interaction of physical objects. Research suggests that when such sounds are heard, the motor networks associated with mirror neurons in the brain respond in a way that allows listeners to experience a sympathetic connection to the sound. These reactions can deepen the connections between musical expressivity and feeling. Composers interested in these sounds as musical material may choose to create one of several types of compositions. Through this project students will learn about six different types of environmental music composition and will work in small groups to create an original work for live or installed performance. Note: Students may work with all six types of compositional techniques or these can be divided into two sets allowing this project to be used twice within one course.

- Set I: Natural instrument, existing sound/scape, and positioned-performance compositions require limited recording and instrument amplification.
- Set II: Manipulated audio, enviro-projection, and conceptual soundscape compositions require more working time with digital audio manipulation software and sound projection systems.

National Arts Standards for Music

Through this lesson, students will have the opportunity to:

- MU:Cr2.1.8a. Select, organize, and document personal musical ideas for arrangements, songs, and compositions within expanded forms that demonstrate tension and release, unity and variety, balance, and convey expressive intent.
- MU:Cr3.1.8a. Evaluate their own work by selecting and applying criteria including appropriate application of compositional techniques, style, form, and use of sound sources.
- MU:Cr3.1.8b. Describe the rationale for refining works by explaining the choices, based on evaluation criteria.
- MU:Cr3.2.8a. Present the final version of their documented personal composition, song, or arrangement, using craftsmanship and originality to demonstrate the application of compositional techniques for creating unity and variety, tension and release, and balance to convey expressive intent.
- MU:Re7.1.6a. Select or choose music to listen to and explain the connections to specific interests or experiences for a specific purpose.
- MU:Re7.2.6a. Describe how the elements of music and expressive qualities relate to the structure of the pieces.
- MU:Re8.1.6a. Describe a personal interpretation of how creators' and performers' application of the elements of music and expressive qualities, within genres and cultural and historical context, convey expressive intent.

- MU:Re9.1.8a. Apply appropriate personally developed criteria to evaluate musical works or performances.
- MU:Cn10.0.8a. Demonstrate how interests, knowledge, and skills relate to personal choices and intent when creating, performing, and responding to music.

Materials

- A set of project *Sketchpages* for each composer.
- Collection of natural objects; assortment of percussion brushes, mallets, and other strikers; instruments as determined by the composers; software or apps suitable for basic recording and digital audio manipulation; projection equipment; spaces for live performance or where sound installations may be placed and visited by an audience.
- Assortment of different notation papers for sketching ideas or notating pieces.
- A *Critical Reflections Guide* for each composer (see appendix B).

Project Time

- This project requires approximately two weeks; eight to ten class periods with some work being completed outside of class.
  - Research phases—two class periods
  - Concept work and gathering of materials/sound sources—three to five days, may be done outside of class
  - Composition work— two to three class periods
  - Performances/installations—time will vary given the nature of the pieces created and where they are to be installed
  - Reflection and Discussion—1 class period

DISCUSSION QUESTIONS TO DEVELOP COMPOSITIONAL CAPACITIES

? Feelingful Intention—The materials used to create environmental compositions can vary significantly from those instruments and voices found in more traditional ensembles. How does this impact setting a feelingful intention?
? Musical Expressivity—Given the unique nature of environmental pieces, are any of the MUSTS "extra important"? What serves to unify these pieces? Does the composer have any control over stability/instability in works where ambient sound can be part of the work?
? Artistic Craftsmanship—This project invites composers to consider auditory parameters, conceptual spaces, performance environment, and temporal spaces in new ways. In what ways is using these elements similar to using elements with which you are more familiar? How is using these elements different?

SEQUENCE OF ACTIVITIES

Phase 1—Surveying the Techniques Used by Composers of Environmental Music

- Introduce this project by asking students to define the term "environmental music." What do they think it is? What ecological sounds can they name? Are they aware of any music that uses sounds from the environment to evoke a particular mood? For example, music used for meditation often contains the sound of flowing water. Can they provide examples of music created to support how a person might experience a fictional environment? A common answer would be videogames. Can they think of any other types of environmental music? (MU:Re7.1.6a)
- Distribute *Sketchpages 1 (Set I) and/or 2 (Set II): Environmental Music Research.* Draw students' attention to the key question, "How do composers of environmental music craft sounds that impact the listener?" Suggest that critically listening to a few different types of environmental music may provide answers.
- As the class works through each example below, encourage students to first consider how they encounter environmental music in the role of listener before trying to determine how composers were able to evoke their responses. Alternately, the class may be divided into six groups with each focused on one type of

environmental composition. Each group can complete their analysis and then report out to the class using a brief excerpt of video to highlight their observations. (MU:Re7.2.6a; MU:Re8.1.6a)

- *Set I: Natural Instrument Composition:* Composers use natural materials such as rocks, trees, grass and water, or man-made materials such as artificial grass, brick, concrete, and plastics to achieve different or unexpected timbres. These objects are not designed for maximized sound potential and must be amplified so that they can be heard in live or recorded performance. Though the sound sources are novel, composers often use traditional techniques for crafting their pieces. Christian Wolff's 1969 "Stones" and Pauline Oliveros' "Rock Piece" from 1979, exemplify an expansive range of techniques for manipulating the sound potential of natural stone and concrete. A performance of these works can be seen at https://www.youtube.com/watch?v=KmrDHwFDUQA.
- *Set I: Existing Sound/scapes Composition:* Composers seeking to tightly control how environmental sounds are used may use a technique called "sampling." This allows composers to intentionally select and record sounds to place within their pieces. The piece "Sarnath," created by Chilean composer Felipe Ontondo in 2010, draws on this technique. The piece uses recordings of bells, drums, and chants from sites in India where the Buddha lived and taught. The composer sought to create a sonic environment similar to the states of mind experienced during mediation practice. An excerpt of this work can be found at https://soundcloud.com/search?q=sarnath.
- *Set I: Positioned-Performance Composition:* Composers may choose to position performances of their pieces in environments where natural sounds, including the day-to-day sounds made by humans, will occur. In this approach, termed "compositional indeterminancy," the composer welcomes unscripted sounds into their composition and knows that the resulting music will be different each time the piece is performed. This 2017 recording of "Elevator Music" https://www.youtube.com/watch?v=HMx3f5kCkAI by American composer Elliott Schwartz demonstrates this indeterminancy. Schwartz created multiple strands of music that are performed simultaneously on different floors of a building. Audience members ride the elevator and hear different music as they go up and down, when the doors open and close, and when they decide to disembark and listen before riding again or exiting the building. The audience co-creates the composition through the decisions they make as the piece unfolds.
- *Set II: Manipulated Audio Composition:* Composers can craft musical material by digitally manipulating audio files. Once sounds have been recorded, composers use software to excerpt, alter, and arrange sounds in different ways. The audio recordings made from sampled and/or manipulated materials can then stand on their own as complete compositions or may be used in partnership with live performance. An example of these concepts can be heard in the work of Lebanese composer Tarek Atoui. He built a collection of original instruments and over the course of several months recorded other composers and performers playing them. He then manipulated the recordings and used layering techniques to create the final work. "Reverse Sessions" is a mix of positioned-performance (in the installation, live exploration/performance, and recording phases) and manipulated audio (once recorded and digitally altered). To see and hear how the work came together, see https://vimeo.com/63645668.
- *Set II: Enviro-Projection Composition:* These compositions feature elements of both manipulated audio composition and positioned-performance in that speakers are arranged in a particular space. An intentional feature of these works is that they take on the implications—cultural, emotional, historical, political, religious, social—of the particular space they inhabit. Susan Philipsz created "War Damaged Musical Instruments" in 2015 for the interior of Theseustempels in Vienna's Volksgarten. She secured access to instruments damaged in World War II and made recordings as they were used to perform music that once signaled different military events. Visit https://www.youtube.com/watch?v=Kf2YzuTDVCA to hear her describe this work.
- *Set II: Conceptual Soundscape Composition:* Early work in environmental music composition often focused on how humans experienced real landscapes and ecologies as soundscapes. As the field evolved, composers turned their attention to the exploration of music evocative of nonphysical landscapes. Compositions attempted to mirror the mental experiences of memory recall, dreams, and free associations before giving way to works that seek to impart the experience of total immersion in an imaginary environment. These sounds can be heard in the music of Skyrim https://www.youtube.com/watch?v=hBkcwy-iWt8 by American composer Jeremy Soule. The environmental settings feature soundscapes that range from quiet and reflective to epic and expansive.

Phase 2—Concept Work

- As the class moves toward creating their own compositions, they will need to understand what resources are available to them. Discuss how students might access natural materials and the equipment necessary to play them. Outline the availability of microphones, recording devices, and amplification equipment. If sound installation is possible, what locations will be acceptable (i.e., will not interfere with other school learning environments/or will contribute to such environments, security of equipment, etc.). (MU:Cr2.1.8a)
- Encourage students to take a few minutes to imagine their final products. This step helps students frame a "big picture" for themselves and allows them to balance smaller details with the product end goal. Invite students to brainstorm on the following topics:
  - Should the work convey a message or invite the audience to consider a particular idea? What might some possible messages or ideas be?
  - What experience can be created for audience members? What kinds of experience can audiences have other than sitting and listening?
  - Which of the techniques of environmental composition best fit the project goal? Do you think composers are limited to one technique in this genre or might multiple techniques be used together? How might that work?
  - What sound sources can be used? How will these be accessed?
  - What tools and materials will be needed to create the piece?
- Distribute *Sketchpage 3: Composition Planner*. Each student composer or composition team should complete the questionnaire and then review it with the teacher to confirm that their conceptual plan is feasible given time, materials, people, and space limitations. Be sure to discuss how materials will be gathered, recorded, and manipulated as fits the needs of each project. (MU:Cr3.1.8b)

Phase 3—Gathering Materials

- The work that students complete during this phase will be determined by the nature of their individual projects. Some students may gather physical materials during class time or outside of school. Those working with naturalistic instruments will need time to explore the sounds that can be made with the materials they have amassed. Other students may be recording naturalistic sounds and will need to experiment with recording devices, apps, or software to figure out how they can position or manipulate these recordings. For those working with traditional instruments in specific performance spaces, time may be needed to scout the performance space and to experiment with performer and audience placement.
- When the bulk of the collection and experimentation processes are complete, encourage composers to move to the creation of their composition.

Phase 4—Create the Composition

- Distribute *Sketchpage 4: Composition Process Journal*. As it is natural for the conception of the composition to evolve as students work, encourage them to complete the "Pre-composition Plan" column on Day 1 of their composing process. (MU:Cr2.1.8b) Note: Students will return to this *Sketchpage* once when their compositions are complete to complete the final two columns.
- Sometimes students get stuck on a single idea and are unsure of how to "switch it up" to make their piece longer. Have a few copies of *Sketchpage 5: Working an Idea* available for students who run into this challenge. This *Sketchpage* encourages students to take a single idea and make one or two changes to hear how the idea might evolve. Students will find this tool easy to use with brief ideas but will also become comfortable with applying it to longer stretches of music as they work. (MU:Cr2.1.8a)
- Check in with composers as they work. This is the time to spot students who are struggling. Use the "Ask, don't tell" approach to guide students in thinking critically about their work. (MU:Cr3.1.8a; MU:Cr3.1.8b)
  - Ask students to describe what they are trying to do.
  - Ask students what they think the problem is.
  - Ask students what they have tried to remedy the problem.
  - Ask students if they would like to open a Composers' Circle to get input from others.

- Ask students if they would like a few suggestions to explore—but remind them that they do not have to use suggestions that you provide. If you do provide suggestions, offer at least three (if you offer only one, students will usually use it without considering whether or not it is really what they want). Encourage the students to experiment with these suggestions to determine if any really fit their piece or if any spark a new idea.
  - You can provide answers, but know that solving student problems by offering single "Here you go" solutions can inhibit growth. Students develop new understandings and skills when they are inside the creative struggle and making progress. If all progress has ceased and frustration is setting in, scaffold the student to the next step by asking questions and offering as few suggestions/solutions as possible to get them back on the creative track.
- Discuss with the class how they would like to get feedback during the composition process. Would they like to share their work with another composer/team who is exploring the same techniques that they are using or would they like to have a "Composer Circle" once or twice during the composition process? When should these happen? Working with students to plan these events provides internal deadlines within the process and allows them to table problems to a specific time when they can seek peer and/or teacher input. (MU:Re7.2.6a; MU:Re8.1.6a)
- As each composer/team completes their composition, steer them back to *Sketchpage 4: Composition Process Journal* to complete the "Post-Composition Report" and "Reflection." When all composers/teams have completed this step, take a few minutes to invite the class to share what they have learned through reflecting on their processes. This discussion will illuminate how compositional thoughts and intentions can evolve over the course of a creative process.

Phase 5—Performances/Installations

- Preparation for performance will be technique dependent. Students engaging in live performance will need ample time to rehearse, preferably in the setting where the performance will occur. Composers who are performing their works through recording will not need rehearsal time, but they should play their pieces in the space where they will be shared to solve issues of volume and balance. Similarly, composers whose work will be performed through projection should set up their equipment and walk through the performance space to make sure that the equipment is functioning properly and that their pieces can be heard above/below/in partnership with ambient sounds. (MU:Cr3.2.8a)
- If performances are open to audiences beyond those students in the class, develop a plan for how to publicize the performance or extend an invitation to other students/classes.
- As these pieces tend to be rather unique, video record performances. It may be possible to live stream pieces or to post recordings to a class website for others to view.

Phase 6—Reflection and Self-Assessment

- Take time to reflect on the performances. What worked best? What was the reaction of the audience? Did the informed audience (members of the class that had been studying environmental music) have a different reaction to pieces than other audience members? What types of sound/environment pairings were most impactful? Why?
- The composition process journal entries may serve as documentation of learning, but if further documentation is needed for assessment records, students also may complete the *Critical Reflection Guide* found in the appendix. (MU:Cr3.1.8a; MU:Cr3.1.8b; MU:Re9.1.8a; MU:Cn10.0.8a)

Optional Extension

Phase 2 through Phase 6 of this project may be repeated with students working in different configurations (individually, partnered, in small groups) to introduce new challenges. Students might also choose to explore a different compositional technique or explore different settings in which to perform or project their work. Composers might also explore "re-composition" by creating new works through the manipulation of recordings of other students' pieces. For this project twist, it will be helpful for the original composers to share the stems—isolated musical tracks—used to create their works.

154　　　　　　　　　　　　　　　　　　Chapter 21

Environmental Music Research (Set I)

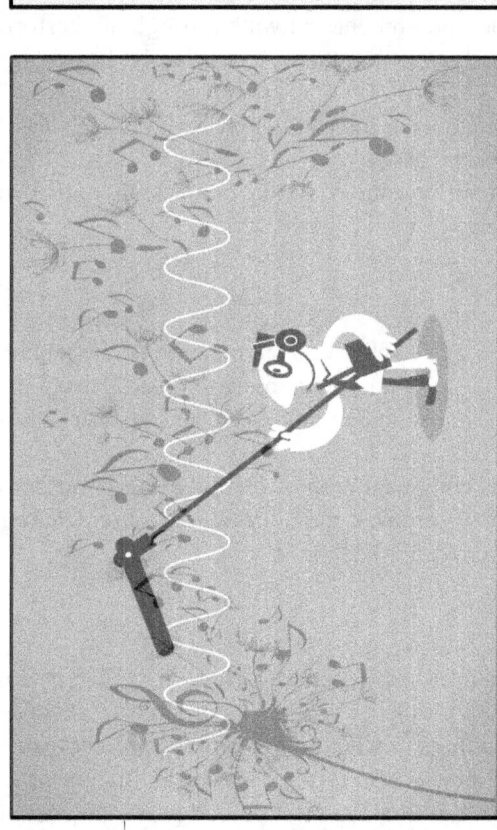

Positioned-Performance Composition
Elliott Schwartz, *Elevator Music*, 1966
https://www.youtube.com/watch?v=HMx3f5kCkAI

1. What do you hear?

2. What mood or feeling does this piece invite for you?

3. How did the composer use these sounds to evoke the reaction you experienced?

Existing Sound/scape Composition
Felipe Ontondo, *Sarnath*, 2010
https://soundcloud.com/search?q=sarnath

1. What do you hear?

2. What mood or feeling does this piece invite for you?

3. How did the composer use these sounds to evoke the reaction you experienced?

Natural Instrument Composition
Christian Wolff, *Stones*, 1969
Pauline Oliveros, *Rock Piece*, 1979
https://www.youtube.com/watch?v=KmrDHwFDUQA

1. What do you hear?

2. What mood or feeling does this piece invite for you?

3. How did the composer use these sounds to evoke the reaction you experienced?

Source: Created by Michele Kaschub and Janice P. Smith with images from iStock/Credit: Maljik and alashi.

Environmental Music Research (Set II)

Conceptual Soundscape Composition
Jeremy Soule, *Skyrim*, 2011
https://www.youtube.com/watch?v=hBkcwy-iWt8

1. What do you hear?
2. What mood or feeling does this piece invite for you?
3. How did the composer use these sounds to evoke the reaction you experienced?

Enviro-Projection Composition:
Susan Philpsz, *War Damaged Instruments*, 2015
https://www.youtube.com/watch?v=Kf2YzuTDVCA

1. What do you hear?
2. What mood or feeling does this piece invite for you?
3. How did the composer use these sounds to evoke the reaction you experienced?

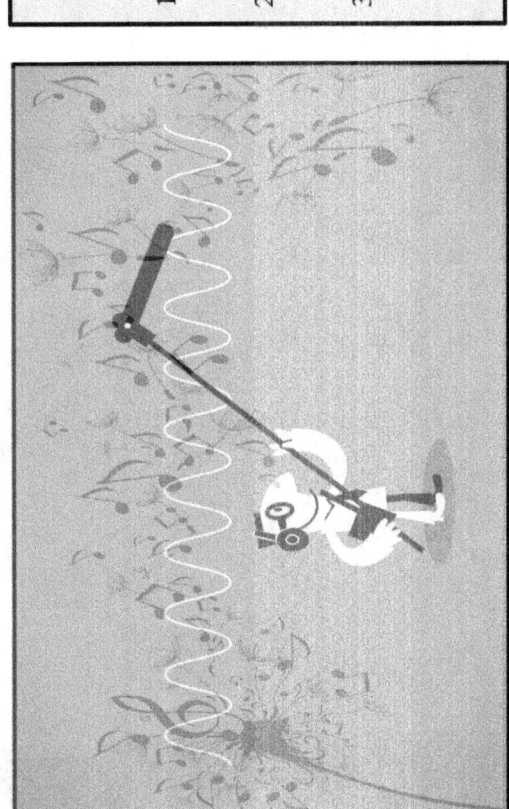

Manipulated Audio Composition
Tarek Atoui, *Reverse Sessions*, 2014
https://vimeo.com/63645668

1. What do you hear?
2. What mood or feeling does this piece invite for you?
3. How did the composer use these sounds to evoke the reaction you experienced?

Source: Created by Michele Kaschub and Janice P. Smith with images from iStock/Credit: Maljik and alashi.

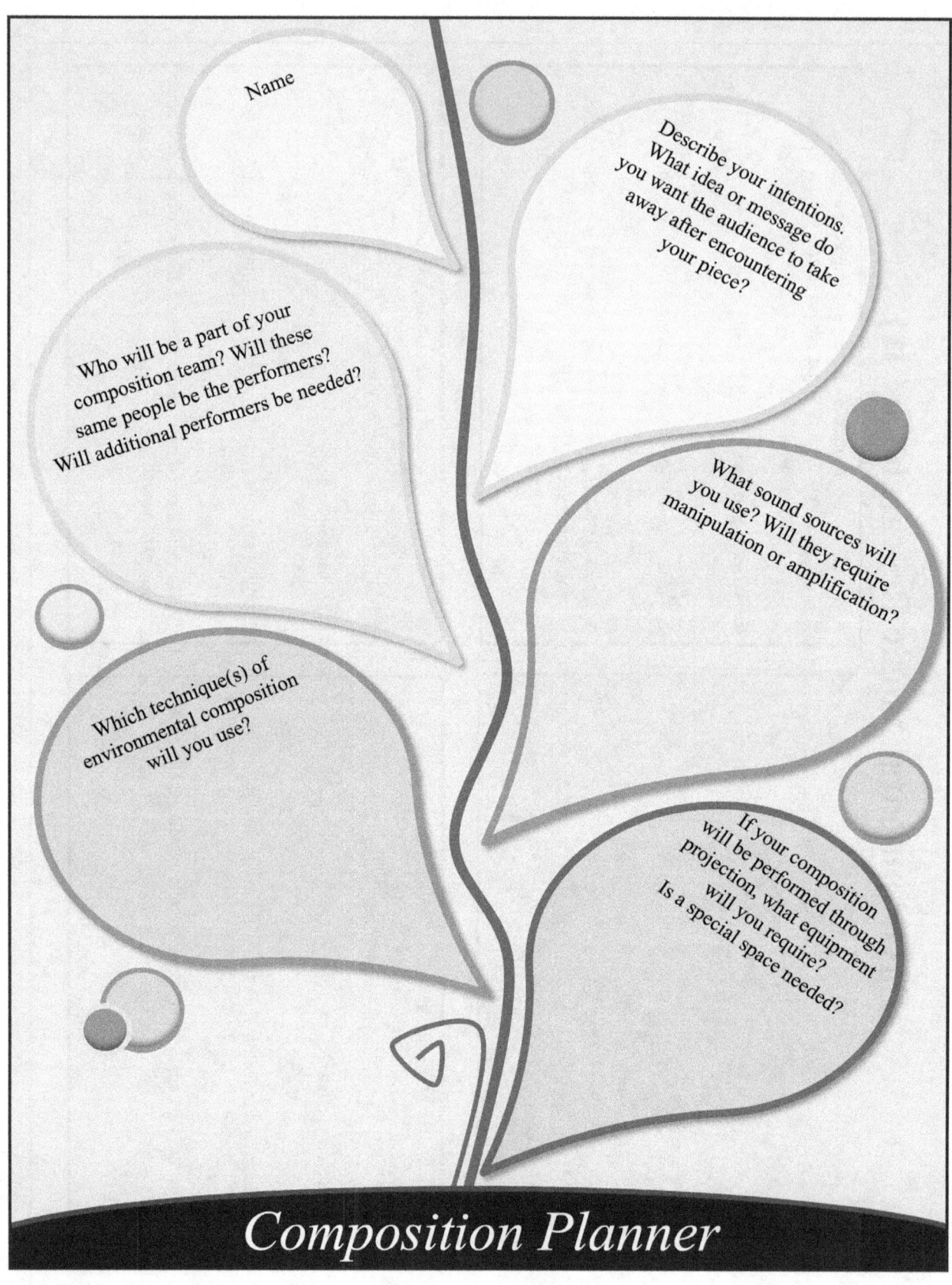

Source: Created by Michele Kaschub and Janice P. Smith.

Composition Process Journal

	Pre-composition Plan	Post-Composition Report	Reflection If there is a difference between your pre- and post-composition notes, please explain.
Feelingful Intention	Describe the feelingful intentions that will focus your work.	What are the feelingful qualities of your finished piece?	
Musical Expressivity	Identify the M.U.S.T.S. pair (or pairs) that will central to the overall affect of your composition. Why is this pair so important?	Which of the M.U.S.T.S. was central to the overall affect of your composition? Why was this pair so impactful?	
Artistic Craftsmanship	List the compositional techniques that you believe have the greatest potential for your piece.	Of the techniques that you used, which had the greatest impact in your piece?	

Source: Created by Michele Kaschub and Janice P. Smith with images from iStock/Credit: archivector.

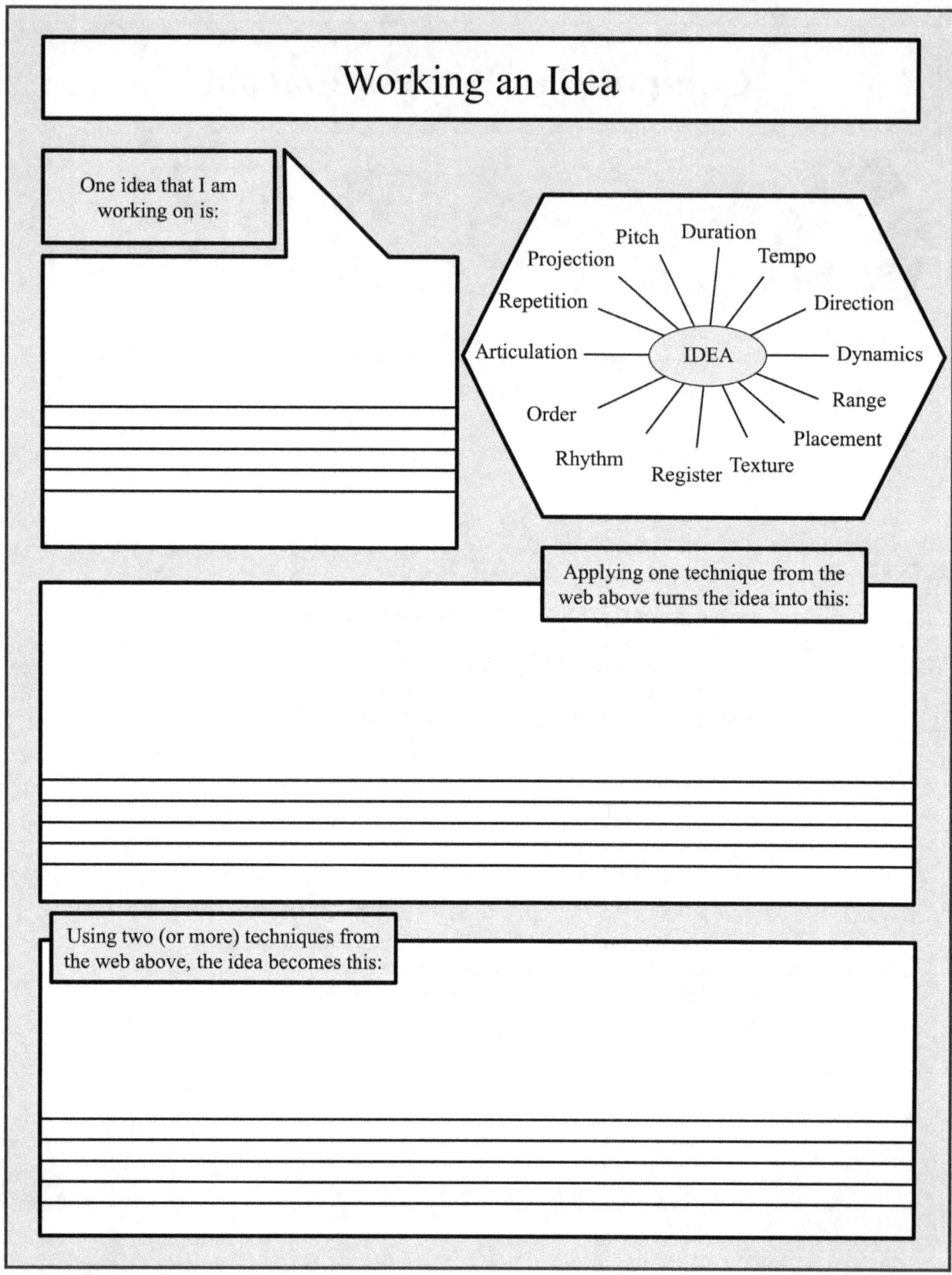

Source: Created by Michele Kaschub and Janice P. Smith.

Chapter 22

Reimagining Great Literature

Advanced Level

Composition Strand: Music Theater

About this Project

Musicals often have a basis in great literature. In this project, students will use a young adult or other novel as the basis for a musical interpretation. The characters propel the composition of songs and the songs become the basis of the musical presentation. While a fully staged production is possible, the intent here is to create a concert version with narration, dialogue and music, but with minimal staging.

National Arts Standards for Music

This lesson presents students with an opportunity to:

- MU:Cr2.1.8a. Select, organize, and document personal musical ideas for arrangements, songs, and compositions within expanded forms that demonstrate tension and release, unity and variety, balance, and convey expressive intent.
- MU:Cr2.1.8b. Use standard and/or iconic notation and/or audio/ video recording to document personal rhythmic phrases, melodic phrases, and harmonic sequences.
- MU:Cr3.1.8a. Evaluate their own work by selecting and applying criteria including appropriate application of compositional techniques, style, form, and use of sound sources.
- MU:Cr3.1.8b. Describe the rationale for refining works by explaining the choices, based on evaluation criteria.
- MU:Re8.1.6a. Describe a personal interpretation of how creators' and performers' application of the elements of music and expressive qualities, within genres and cultural and historical context, convey expressive intent.
- MU:Re9.1.8a. Apply appropriate personally developed criteria to evaluate musical works or performances.
- MU:Cn10.0.8a. Demonstrate how interests, knowledge, and skills relate to personal choices and intent when creating, performing, and responding to music.

Materials

- A set of *Sketchpages* for each composer
- A collection of young adult or other novels with strong character-driven plots
- Instruments (guitar, keyboards, or digital sound sources)
- Notation software or staff paper
- A *Critical Reflections Guide* for each composer (see appendix B)

Project Time

This project will take eight to ten class periods to complete. The composing component of the project will take six to eight sessions. The number of sessions needed to rehearse and present the performance will vary depending on presentation format and available rehearsal time.

DISCUSSION QUESTIONS TO DEVELOP COMPOSITIONAL CAPACITIES

? Feelingful Intention—As each of the characters in the story fill different roles in advancing the storyline, so will each of the songs serve different functions within the musical. What feelingful intention seems right for each song? How do these feelingful intentions create a dramatic arch that builds and then resolves across the full set of songs?

? Musical Expressivity—Identify those MUSTS that will be most impactful in shaping the emotional journey of each song and across the full set of songs. It is particularly important to consider what will provide unity within the show.

? Artistic Craftsmanship—What compositional techniques will be used to evoke a feelingful response to the individual character songs? How will techniques be varied between songs to maintain the audience's interest? What sound sources are best suited for the overall nature of the story?

SEQUENCE OF ACTIVITIES

Phase 1—Novel Selection and Storyboarding

- Working with the entire class, select a novel and create a storyboard. Begin by creating a list of familiar novels that might be suitable for reframing as a musical. (MU:Cr 2.1.8a) Give careful attention to the importance of the characters. A story which relies heavily on action (i.e., high-speed car chases and space battles) may be difficult to transition into song form. Conversely, such a musical could be very exciting! Discuss what makes the story interesting and why an audience might be attracted to it as a musical.
- List the characters and identify key moments in the story.
- Create a storyboard using the *Storyboarding Sketchpage*. Project this page or distribute copies to students.

Phase 2—Creation of Character Songs

- Have the class form songwriting teams based on the number of songs identified during the creation of the storyboard.
- Each team will need a copy of the *Creating Character Songs Sketchpage*.
- Songwriters will need to consider:
  - The nature of their character. Is the character funny, serious, innocent, devious, and so on?
  - What the audience needs to know about this character?
  - What this character needs to share with the audience to advance the storyline?
  - What type of song (I am, ballad, charm, comedic, duet, trio, ensemble, or other) the character will present?
- Using the ideas on the *Sketchpage*, create the song. Some composers prefer to create lyrics first while others create chord patterns or melodies—and sometimes all of this happens at once! Any approach that allows the team to create their song is appropriate. (MU:Cr2.1.8a)
- Create a lead sheet for the song with lyrics, melody and chords notated. Be ready to assist with notation or finding just the right chord as student work. (MU:Cr2.1.8b)
- Practice performing this draft of the song to share in the preliminary run-through.

Phase 3—Preliminary Run-Through and Composer Circle

- Once most of the composers are finished, it is helpful to do a preliminary run-through or two to see how the production is shaping up and to allow ample opportunities for revision. All of the guidelines for Composers' Circles (see pp. 40–41) should be reviewed with particular emphasis on critiquing the work and not the performance or the composers. Focusing on the capacities and the ideas on the character *Sketchpages* can assist with this. (MU:Re8.1.6a)
- Focus on the story and how the music reveals the characters and moves the plot forward. Each composing group should maintain artistic control of their work and decide whether to accept or reject any suggestions from the group. (MU:Cr3.1.8a)
- Once a run-through has happened, allow the groups time to make any revisions they decide are necessary and to create any additional music that may be needed. (MU:Cr3.1.8b)
- Another run-through will be needed before rehearsals can begin. The goal is to have most major revisions done before beginning rehearsals. However, minor editing likely will occur throughout performance preparation.

Phase 4—Rehearsal and Performance

- Decide who will perform what parts of the production. Will the composers do it or will a class member be cast in that role and perform the song? It is wise to leave this decision until this point, so that composers are writing for a specific character, rather than a specific person. What parts, if any, involve the whole class?
- The teacher should serve as the director but employ a facilitation model to draw ideas from students. This approach will maintain efficiency and preserve students' sense of ownership in their work.
- Run through the production a few times without any staging or actions. Once this flows easily from one section to the next, consider whether to add any minor action such as walkovers or standing and sitting.
- Continue rehearsals, adding staging and other theatrical elements, until the performance is polished and ready to share.
- Perform for a live audience. If at all possible, perform more than once so that students can become comfortable in their roles. Open each presentation with students describing their creative process and guiding the audience to pay attention to particularly interesting musical moments.

Phase 5—Reflection and Self-Assessment

- Have all composers and participants complete the *Critical Reflection Guide* found in the appendix. (MU:Cr3.1.8a; MU:Cr3.1.8b; MU:Re9.1.8a; MU:Cn10.0.8a)

Optional Extension

One possible extension is to fully stage the show. If the teacher and class decide to do this, it is best to form a student-based production company where students are in charge of the publicity, costume design, makeup, lighting, set design, stage-managing, and so on. There should also be a student production manager and a student director. Specific people should be actors and musicians. Each student should have a role in the company. It may be wise to have them apply for the two or three jobs they would most like to have and to audition for the various roles. Ownership of the performance should be vested in the students. Adults should allow them to solve any resulting problems or issues with minimal intervention.

Creating Character Songs

Character name: _____
How would you describe this character? Are they funny, serious, innocent, devious, etc.?

What does the audience need to know about this character?

What does this character need to share with the audience to advance the storyline?

What type of song should this character present? (I am, ballad, charm, comedic, or other) Why?

How will this song sound? What is the mood at the opening? Will the verses and choruses be the same or will they contrast in some way? Sketch your ideas here:

Source: Created by Michele Kaschub and Janice P. Smith with images from iStock/Credit: Sudowoodo.

Storyboard

Beginning: Is there a musical introduction or narrator?

Create a list of songs and any other music that is needed.

Determine what happens between songs. Is there narration? Who delivers these lines, the narrator or one of the characters? Is narration needed between each song or might some songs happen back-to-back?

How will the production end? Will there be a "big finish" song with all of the characters, an ensemble number, an instrumental finale, or something else?

Source: Created by Michele Kaschub and Janice P. Smith with images from iStock/Credit: Sudowoodo.

Song Lead Sheet

Write the lyrics and chords for your song here:

Source: Created by Michele Kaschub and Janice P. Smith with images from iStock/Credit: Sudowoodo.

Appendix A: Notation Templates

Title:
Composer(s):

for composers using invented or iconograhic notation

Appendix A.1 **Staff Paper for Invented or Iconographic Scores.** *Source*: Created by Michele Kaschub and Janice P. Smith.

Title:
Composer(s):

for composers using invented or iconograhic notation in partnership with traditional notation (best for use as a memory booster before part alignment is desired)

Appendix A.2 **Staff Paper for Combined Scoring Styles.** *Source*: Created by Michele Kaschub and Janice P. Smith.

Appendix A.3 Staff Paper for Aligning Parts in Combined Scoring Styles. *Source:* Created by Michele Kaschub and Janice P. Smith.

for composers using invented or iconograhic notation in partnership with traditional notation (best for use when part alignment is needed)

Title:
Composer(s):

for composers using traditional notation

Appendix A.4 Five Line Staff Paper. *Source*: Created by Michele Kaschub and Janice P. Smith.

Appendix B: Critical Reflection and Composer Feedback Guides

Critical Reflection Guide

Composition Title:_____ Name: _____

What did I learn from this composition project?

FI-ME-AC Connections

I/We used *(an element or tool of Artistic Craftsmanship)*
to invite the perception of *(Musical Expressivity/single M.U.S.T.S)*
which is meant to evoke the feeling of *(Feelingful Intention)*.

1. I/We used _____
to invite the perception of _____
which is meant to evoke the feeling of _____.

2. I/We used _____
to invite the perception of _____
which is meant to evoke the feeling of _____.

3. I/We used _____
to invite the perception of _____
which is meant to evoke the feeling of _____.

4. I/We used _____
to invite the perception of _____
which is meant to evoke the feeling of _____.

5. I/We used _____
to invite the perception of _____
which is meant to evoke the feeling of _____.

Evaluation

This composition is…
☐ amazing (4) because…
☐ successful (3) because…
☐ acceptable (2) because…
☐ promising (1) because…

What would I do differently if I were to repeat this project?

Other important thoughts I have learned about music or music composition.

Source: Created by Michele Kaschub and Janice P. Smith.

Composer Feedback

Title: _____
Composer(s): _____

	Critic 1:	Critic 2:	Critic 3:
👏👏👏👏 Bravo!			
👏👏👏👏 Bravo!			
An idea to consider			
An idea to consider			

What, if any, ideas for revision did you take from this feedback?

Source: Created by Michele Kaschub and Janice P. Smith.

Index

"Acra Sacra", 142
activities: individual, 3, 35, 51, 107, 114, 144, 152; partnered, 3, 31, 153; small group, 3, 16, 28, 31, 40, 44, 51, 65, 67, 73, 74, 80, 92, 123, 149, 153; whole class, 28, 80, 133, 161
anchor charts, 39
aptitude, 15
Arnold, Malcolm, 142
articulation techniques, 26
artistic craftsmanship, 4, 15, 20–21, 26, 28, 29, 31, 42, 44, 52, 60, 62, 70, 74, 80, 92, 98, 106, 113–14, 122–23, 130, 142, 143, 150, 160
artistic purpose, 4, 16, 44
artistic thinking, 20, 113
audience: experience of, 22, 31, 36, 44, 48, 51, 114, 152, 160; perceptions of, 23, 67, 71, 99; reactions of, 39, 41, 44, 62, 66, 74, 75, 92, 115, 123, 131, 133
autonomy: artistic, 3, 4, 9, 113; compositional, 53; musical, 9, 11, 35

Bach, J.S., 142
Bruner, Jerome, 35

canon, 26
Cello Suite No. 1, "Gigue", 142
choral arrangements, 122
collaborative learning, 3, 115, 144
communication skills, 39
composer's circles, 3, 40–41, 62, 99, 141, 144, 161
composer's sketchbook, 3, 27
composer's voice, 3, 4, 113
composers: characteristics of, 9; interviewing, 141–44; peer interaction, 3, 9, 10, 16, 39, 40, 42, 61–62, 82, 92, 99, 105, 113, 122, 133, 143, 153; and reluctance to share work, 42
composing: for characters, 48, 80–81, 159–61; in digital media, 47–48, 69–72, 82, 105–12, 149–58; electronic music, 3, 19, 25, 48, 69–72, 82, 105–12, 149–58; instrumental music, 3, 10, 47–48, 65–68, 97–105; for music theater, 3, 47–48, 73–76, 79, 81, 113–18, 159–61; and songwriting, 36–37, 47–48, 51–58, 79–90, 106, 121–28, 160; for video games, 150; and visual media, 48, 62
compositional capacities, 11, 15, 20, 26, 28, 30–31, 38–39, 42, 52, 60, 66, 70, 74, 80, 91, 92, 98, 99, 106, 122, 130, 142–44, 150, 160–61
compositional task, 3, 20, 28, 35, 37
compositions: providing feedback about, 3, 31, 35, 39–42, 62, 82, 98–99, 115, 122, 133, 144, 153, 169; sharing, 3–4, 9–11, 15–16, 35, 37–42, 53, 71, 74, 93, 108, 115, 123, 133, 143
Couf, Herbert, 142
creativity, blocks to, 37

Davis, Stuart, 65
Dewey, John, 33
digital media, 48, 69–72, 105–12, 149–58
dynamics, techniques for, 23–24

electronic music, 69–72, 105–12, 149–58
enduring understandings, 3
essential questions, 3
etudes, 21–26
expressive potentials, 3, 98

"Fantasy for Trumpet", 142
feedback: application of, 39, 53, 62, 99; constructive, 3, 11, 62, 133, 144; receptivity to, 40–42, 62, 82, 92, 99, 133, 153
feelingful intention, 4, 9, 10, 15–17, 20, 26–29, 36–37, 41–42, 44, 52, 60, 62, 66, 70, 74, 80, 92–93, 98, 106–8, 114–15, 122–23, 130, 142
film scoring, 47, 59–64, 91–96, 129–40
Folio, Cynthia, 142
form, techniques for, 24

graphic organizer, 3, 11, 30–31
"Gravity", 65
guiding questions, 28, 37–38, 42, 47, 52, 60, 66, 70, 74, 80, 92, 98, 106, 114, 122, 130, 142–43, 150, 160

harmony, 21, 26, 65
Hines, Earl, 65

idea development, 4, 7–9, 31
idea extension, 31, 37
idea generation, 9, 15, 31, 37–38
imagination, 15, 20, 27, 31, 36–37, 48
inner hearing, 20
instability, 16, 19, 42, 92, 150
instrumental works, 3, 10, 47–48, 65–68, 82, 97–105, 141–8
instrumentation and orchestration, techniques for, 25
instruments, 9, 16, 19, 20, 25, 37, 39, 48, 66–67, 70–71, 73–74, 80, 91, 98, 100, 115, 122, 130, 133, 142–43, 150–52, 159
"Introduction, Dance and Furioso", 142
introductions, verbal, 16

Kandinsky, Wassily, 65

lead sheets, 121–23, 160
listening, 16, 21, 35, 38, 52–53, 66, 74, 82, 108
"Lucky", 65
lyrics, creation of, 16, 23, 36, 51, 53, 82, 105, 122, 160

Mayer, John, 65
McCraken, Melissa, 65
melody, creation of, 21–22, 35, 51, 122, 160
motif, 15
motion, 16, 18–21, 70, 74, 92, 130, 142
music, elements of, 18–20, 51, 59, 65–66, 69, 73, 79, 97–98, 105, 113, 121–22, 129, 132, 141–42, 150–51, 159–60
musical expressivity, 4, 15–16, 19–20, 26–27, 29, 52, 60, 66, 70, 74, 80, 92, 98, 106, 114, 122, 130, 142–43, 149, 150, 160
music theater, 3, 47–48, 73–76, 79, 81, 113–18, 159–64
music theory, 4, 20
M.U.S.T.S. use of, 16, 18–20, 26, 28, 31, 36, 38–39, 52, 60, 66–67, 70–71, 75, 80, 92–93, 106, 108, 114, 122, 130, 142, 150, 160

National Core Music Standards, 3–7, 51, 59, 65, 69, 73, 79, 91, 97, 105, 113, 121, 129, 141, 149, 159
notation: need for, 27, 67, 74; types of, 20, 27, 150; working with, 26–27, 51, 69, 73, 91, 98, 121–22, 129–30, 133, 141, 159–60

Orchestration. *See* instrumentation and orchestration, techniques for
Ostinato, 22, 30

Paul Dresher Ensemble, 98
peers: feedback from, 3, 39–42, 62, 82, 99, 122, 133; works of, 3, 10, 16, 39–42, 105, 113, 133, 153
Piaget, Jean, 35
pitch, techniques for, 21–22
principle pairs, 18, 28

Radiohead, 65
reflection, 16, 42, 53, 62, 67, 71, 75, 83, 93, 100, 108, 115, 123, 133, 141, 144, 153, 161
release, 16, 19–20, 26, 30, 42, 51, 59, 65, 69–70, 73, 79, 91, 97, 105, 113–14, 129, 132, 141, 149, 159
repetition, 18, 20, 52, 70
revision, 42, 62, 161
rhythm, 18–19, 22, 24, 26, 30, 38, 51, 65, 69, 73, 82, 91, 97, 105–6, 112–13, 122, 142
Rite of Spring, 65
Rózsa, Miklós, 142

silence, 10, 16, 18–19, 42, 74
Sketchpages: introduction to, 3, 27; teaching with, 27–31, 52; use of, 11, 31
social media, 3, 37, 48, 59, 61–62, 113, 151
software for looping, 130, 133
"Sonatina para clarinet solo", 142
songwriting, 36–37, 48, 51–58, 79–90, 121–28, 160
sonify, 73–74
sound, emotional impact, 9–10, 15, 51, 115, 151
sound effects, 93
space, techniques for, 22–23
stability, 16, 19, 42, 92, 150
stasis, 16, 18, 20, 42, 74
Stravinsky, Igor, 65
student autonomy, 3–4, 11, 35, 53, 113
student ownership, 9, 16, 35, 92, 161
Suite for Unaccompanied Tuba, "Galop" and "Presto", 142
synesthesia, 65

task, compositional, 3, 20, 28, 37
techniques, for: articulation, 26; canon, 26; dynamics, 23–24; form, 24; instrumentation, 24–25; orchestration, 24–25; pitch, 21–22; space, 22–23; texture, 25–26; theme and variations 59, 69, 97; time, 22
tempo, 19, 22, 65, 105, 150
tension, 16, 19–20, 30, 37, 42, 51, 53, 59, 62, 67, 69, 70, 73–75, 79, 83, 91–93, 97, 100, 105, 108, 133–35
texture, techniques of, 25–26
timbre. *See* tone color
time, techniques for, 22
tone color, 19, 35
tools, 16, 20

unity, 16, 18–20, 30, 39, 42, 51–52, 59, 62, 65, 69, 73, 79, 91, 97, 105, 113, 129, 141, 149, 159, 160

variety, 16, 18–20, 30, 39, 42, 51, 59, 62, 65, 69, 73, 79, 91, 97, 105, 113, 129, 141, 149, 159

Waller, "Fats", 65

Zerkel, David, 142

About the Authors

Michele Kaschub is professor of music and director of Music Teacher Education in the Osher School of Music at the University of Southern Maine. Her scholarly interests include children's composition, composition pedagogy, choral music education, curriculum design and assessment, and the professional development of teachers at all levels. She is coauthor of *Minds on Music: Composition for Creative and Critical Thinking, Experiencing Music Composition in Grades 3–5*, and coeditor of *Composing Our Future: Preparing Music Educators to Teach Composition, Promising Practices in 21st Century Music Teacher Education* and *Experiencing Music Composition in Grades K–2*. She has contributed chapters to several books and numerous articles to professional journals. She is the immediate past chair and academic editor of *Music Educators Journal* (a journal of the National Association for Music Education) and editor of the *Oxford Handbook of Music Composition Pedagogy*. An active clinician and guest lecturer, she has presented papers and workshops at colleges and conferences in California, Colorado, Connecticut, Delaware, Florida, Georgia, Illinois, Kansas, Maine, Maryland, Massachusetts, Michigan, Minnesota, New Hampshire, New Jersey, New York, North Carolina, Oregon, Pennsylvania, Rhode Island, South Carolina, Tennessee, Texas, Utah, Vermont, and Virginia, as well as internationally in Canada, England, Ireland, and Germany.

Janice P. Smith is professor of music education at the Aaron Copland School of Music, Queens College, City University of New York. She teaches courses in general music, foundations of music education, composition pedagogy, and music methods for elementary teachers. She previously had a thirty-year career as a general music specialist in the Maine public schools. Her writings have appeared in the *Music Educators Journal, General Music Today, Research Studies in Music Education,* and *Music Education Research International*. She has presented sessions at state, national, and international music education conferences. She is coauthor with Michele Kaschub of *Minds on Music: Composition for Creative and Critical Thinking, Experiencing Music Composition in Grades K-2,* and *Experiencing Music Composition in Grades 3–5*. She is coeditor, with Kaschub, of *Composing Our Future: Preparing Music Educators to Teach Composition* and *Promising Practices in 21st Century Music Teacher Education*.

www.ingramcontent.com/pod-product-compliance
Lightning Source LLC
Chambersburg PA
CBHW060253240426
43673CB00047B/1915